Bayview

Bayview

Solved

Solved

HOW THE WORLD'S
GREAT CITIES
ARE FIXING
THE CLIMATE CRISIS

David Miller

ÆVO UTP

Aevo UTP
An imprint of University of Toronto Press
Toronto Buffalo London
utorontopress.com
© University of Toronto Press 2020

Library and Archives Canada Cataloguing in Publication

Title: Solved : how the world's great cities are fixing the climate crisis / David Miller.
Names: Miller, David, 1958–, author.
Description: Includes bibliographical references and index.
Identifiers: Canadiana (print) 20200285424 | Canadiana (ebook) 20200285491 |
   ISBN 9781487506827 (cloth) | ISBN 9781487534905 (PDF) | ISBN 9781487534912 (EPUB)
Subjects: LCSH: Urban ecology (Sociology) – Case studies. | LCSH: City planning –
   Climatic factors – Case studies. | LCSH: Sustainable urban development – Case studies. |
   LCSH: Climate change mitigation – Case studies. | LCSH: Urban policy – Case studies.
Classification: LCC HT241 .M55 2020 | DDC 307.76 – dc23

ISBN 978-1-4875-0682-7 (cloth)   ISBN 978-1-4875-3491-2 (EPUB)
                                   ISBN 978-1-4875-3490-5 (PDF)

Printed in Canada

The Mrs. Joan H. Miller Scholarship Fund is the recipient of royalties from *Solved*. Its scholarships are awarded annually to single mothers and others returning to post-secondary education. All money raised goes directly to the award of scholarships, and through a matching program the fund has generated more than $250,000 to date. For details, see https://torontofoundation.ca/listings/mrs_joan_h_miller_scholarship_fund.

We acknowledge the financial support of the Government of Canada, the Canada Council for the Arts, and the Ontario Arts Council, an agency of the Government of Ontario, for our publishing activities.

**Canada Council
for the Arts**

**Conseil des Arts
du Canada**

ONTARIO ARTS COUNCIL
CONSEIL DES ARTS DE L'ONTARIO
an Ontario government agency
un organisme du gouvernement de l'Ontario

Funded by the
Government
of Canada

Financé par le
gouvernement
du Canada

Canadä

MIX
Paper from
responsible sources
FSC
www.fsc.org **FSC® C016245**

Contents

Foreword

I first began really thinking about cities and climate change back in the 1990s, when I spent some months in Curitiba, Brazil. This provincial city should be on every traveler's list, and not just because it's on the way to Iguazu Falls. It shows what happens when city leaders truly set their minds to making change. Mayor Jaime Lerner pioneered many developments, from vast parkland expansion for flood control to a huge system of municipal bike paths to – crucially – the first instances of what we now call bus rapid transit. And in the process he created a city where people really enjoyed living: when he left office because of term limits, his popularity topped 90 per cent.

Making change in national capitols is crucial – but it's also slow, and hard. The lobbying power of incumbent industries, especially those involved in fossil fuels, is often strongest in federal congresses and parliaments, and so when change comes it often comes too slowly. Also, many national legislatures give extra power to shrinking rural areas, meaning that these regions can veto change. Cities, by contrast, are nimbler and often inhabited by more progressive, younger, and more gregarious citizens. And the people who run them are much closer to the issues that matter. So it's been truly encouraging to watch the C40 Cities emerge as a key part of the effort to bend the carbon curve and change the outcome of the climate drama.

As this fine volume makes clear, the opportunities are enormous (and never more so than now, when the COVID-19 crisis has opened our minds to the possibility of inhabiting our great urban areas in new ways). We see, just in the last few years, cities such as London and Paris moving decisively to shift their transit mix toward buses and muscles; we see cities such as New York standing up to landlords by forcing them to retrofit existing buildings for energy efficiency. (The landlords will end up thanking them, as energy costs drop sharply.) We see cities outlawing gas connections for new constructions and making deals with utilities to provide renewable power. And, happily, we see cities figuring out how to put pressure on the larger systems of our society: the widespread move to divest civic pensions from the fossil fuel industry, and now to pressure banks that do business with municipalities to stop lending to businesses that operate within this industry, will play a large role in reordering power at the national and global levels.

All of this will not only help to ward off sea-level rise and forestall more giant storms – it will make for better, cooler, cleaner, happier, more resilient cities. And ones that are more fun too!

Bill McKibben
Senior advisor, 350.org
June 2020

Preface

People know something is seriously wrong. At the end of 2019, unprecedented and out-of-control wildfires burned outside Los Angeles. Blazes were ravaging the Amazon. Australian wildfires, born from drought and searing temperatures above 40°C (over 110°F), raged. The world watched as thousands of people fled their homes, millions of acres of eucalyptus forest were destroyed, and hundreds of thousands of animals lost their habitat. Koala bears were given bottled water from passing humans, their only chance of survival. An estimated one billion more animals were not so lucky.

At the same time, in another part of the world, there were unprecedented floods in Jakarta. Scores dead and tens of thousands of people were displaced. It's the second such disaster in a few years, in a capital city that is sinking – literally. It is so serious that the president of Indonesia has announced that the capital must be moved. As of December 31, 2019, Jakarta, the heart of a region of 30 million people, had a population estimated at 10.8 million.

And then there is Houston, Texas, the world capital of the oil industry. On Friday, August 25, 2017, Hurricane Harvey, a storm of extraordinary intensity, made landfall. Over the ensuing four days, a year's worth of rain fell on Houston – as much as fifty inches. The flooding was massive and unprecedented. Estimates were a trillion gallons of rainfall, which seems impossible to picture because it is so much. In a major rainfall event of this size, the land cannot absorb the water – it is like a sponge that is full. Nor can the human systems. They are built for normal, predictable events that happen every fifty or one hundred years. This was a once-in-five-hundred-years storm.

People know about the wildfires and about Hurricane Harvey. What they might not know is that the extreme drought and hot weather in Australia that create the conditions for out-of-control wildfires are now happening every year. They also might not know that in 2015, 2016, 2018, and 2019 Houston also had severe flooding events, two more of which were at the threshold of a once-in-five-hundred-years storm. What was once rare has become normal.

As of mid-2020, the world is in the midst of a global pandemic, COVID-19. While the science is still developing, it seems clear that the impact of COVID-19 has been far more serious in places with significant air-quality issues – typically caused by pollutants and processes similar to those that are causing climate change. In addition, there is evidence that environmental destruction – which worsens climate change – contributes to the increased risk of global health challenges, such as Ebola, MERS, and now COVID-19. At the same time, extreme weather events have not disappeared: in May, for example, extreme rainfall in Michigan caused a dam to burst and the massive flooding of Midland, a town of more than forty thousand people. The precipitating event was a once-in-five-hundred-years storm – the second within the last five years.

Scientists have been warning us about such events for a very long time – a changing climate has the ability to devastate people and nature. And the potential consequences are serious indeed. In Africa, for example, predictions are that the loss of arable land could cause tens of millions of people to become migrants – climate migrants. Where will they go? We have already seen the world struggle to cope with refugees from Syria. How can our political systems handle tens of millions of migrants? Where will they live? What will they eat?

The knowledge of the serious consequences of climate change brought scientists and governments together in 1988 in Toronto, Canada – where I live – for the Toronto Conference on the Changing Atmosphere. The conference did not quite reach agreement on a path forward, but it helped spur the international community to address climate change. In 1992, the United Nations Framework Convention on Climate Change was entered into, which came into force as a binding treaty agreement on March 21, 1994, by which time a sufficient number of nations (now 197) had ratified the treaty. The framework set nonbinding limits on greenhouse gas emissions for the signatory nations and agreed on a process – known annually as a conference of the parties (or COP) – to find ways to implement the treaty. In 1997 in Kyoto, Japan, the parties were successful in agreeing to a protocol that set limits for developed countries – generally speaking, as a first target, to reduce by approximately 6 per cent by 2012 based on 1990 levels of greenhouse gas emissions, followed by further reduction commitments. Subsequently, intergovernmental action, except for Europe, waned – Canada, under a right-wing, pro-oil government, abandoned the Kyoto Protocol; the United States never ratified it.

Against this backdrop, twenty years of negotiations through a series of COPs passed. Twenty years. In 2015, led by the United States and China, nations finally reached agreement at COP21 in Paris on a program of action against climate change. It was generally known at the time that the agreement was not strong enough – but most advocates believed that the fact of agreement could help build momentum for the necessary change. There was euphoria then – but today, five years later, we know that events have not upheld that optimism.

The latest science is clear, and daunting. The likelihood of dangerous climate change is accelerating. The conclusions of both the Intergovernmental Panel on Climate Change and the United States National Climate Assessment are definite: climate change is human caused. Its implications on human life and on nature are exceptionally serious. And the measures currently undertaken by national governments are woefully insufficient to hold overall average temperature increases to 1.5 degrees, the scientifically deter-mined threshold past which serious risk to planetary health occurs. The United States has announced a planned withdrawal from the Paris Accord, and even the actions of Canada, who led the charge in Paris for a high ambition of a 1.5 degree limit to global heating, are not remotely sufficient to contribute to its share of the necessary reductions in greenhouse gas emissions.

Those facts should not be news to many. It has been clear to anyone who sees the news that the world is heating faster than orig-inally expected, and that national governments are not taking the need to act nearly seriously enough. People sense this. Some are discouraged; others are angry at the elected officials who seem to listen too much to the fossil fuel lobby and not enough to science. Their feelings are understandable – but there is another story – one that gives reasons for hope.

That story is what is happening in the world's major cities, where activist mayors of different political backgrounds are taking bold and effective actions that are dramatically reducing greenhouse gas emissions.

Why Cities?

"Why cities?" is a question I am often asked. And to someone who has spent more than thirty years involved in municipal politics, it's a question that makes little sense, because to me it is obvious why cities are acting on climate change: because they can. And they must.

First of all, the world is now more urban than not – and this is a relatively recent change. In the first decade of this century, for the first time in the history of human civilization, urban populations surpassed rural. From the beginning of civilization, humans were predominately rural agrarian populations – but no longer. And the trend to urbanization is only growing more pronounced as popula-tions in China and India move to urban areas from rural. The world is getting increasingly urban, and this century will be defined by this historic change.

City governments have different structures and powers in different countries. But there are significant similarities. Almost always they are responsible for planning – for setting a future vision for the city and making the rules about what types and sizes of buildings can be built and where. Where will industry go? Commercial buildings like offices and shops? Single-family houses? Apartments? Parks? Schools?

This power to set where and how buildings will be built is often accompanied by the power to regulate or the ability to influence the type of building to be built through building codes. These codes set the material and other standards for the buildings and are detailed and powerful as they set the rules for an entire industry.

There is one other crucially important thing about the responsibility for planning – by law, city governments are required to consult with residents about the city plan (in Canada these are called official plans – the overall vision for the city – this term will be used here for convenience) and individual development applications. As a result, city governments have developed robust resident engagement processes that give local residents a very real say over decisions that affect their lives and their neighborhoods. There is a lively, robust, and extremely healthy local democracy, in which the voices of local residents are heard, and they can and do participate in decisions made by city hall – well beyond planning. One of the results of this healthy local democracy is that elected members of city council tend to be grassroots politicians, who regularly engage and listen to people and vote with the expressed wishes of their constituents at the forefront of their minds.

Furthermore, the responsibilities of cities lead to a direct and obvious connection to environmental issues. Cities are responsible for parks. For trees. For housing. For public transportation. For water and sewers. Waste management. For income support, economic development, and public health. Often for schools and education as well – in short, for the services that affect people's everyday lives the most. And many of these responsibilities have a significant impact on the environment – or allow the city to have a significant impact on the environment, if it chooses. For example, public health authorities will have a responsibility for air quality as poor air is a significant health issue. Clean water and waste management have direct links to environmental issues; as a result, cities have for a very long time been responsible for and acted against environmental challenges.

The final point is of tremendous importance: in most of the world cities have a directly elected mayor or governor, ultimately having overall responsibility for the city government – for its plans, policies, and actions. The role of a mayor can be instrumental and transformative for a city; because of the dual responsibility for both the development and detailed implementation of policy, there is a tremendous potential for effective action by city governments. And there is a history of such actions – we take sewers and clean water for granted in North American cities, but sewers originally were a public health response to significant outbreaks of disease, particularly in low-income communities, resulting from the use of open sewers for human waste. A history of activist policies combined with effective actions (often with social justice implications) is embedded in the history and DNA of cities.

Mayors and Climate Change

Why are mayors interested in climate change? First of all, many simply recognize the moral, ethical, and practical urgency in addressing climate change. Others are smart politicians who listen to the voters. But most of all, the mayors of the world's great cities are acting on climate change because they must. Cities are already experiencing the impact of climate change, and unlike national governments, mayors cannot wait to act. Mayors have a unique combination of the compulsion to address this issue – because of their residents' expectation of action – and the ability to act.

Cities that have been hit by super storms, such as Houston, New York, and New Orleans, do not have the luxury of debating whether climate change is real. The mayors of those cities needed to lead both the reconstruction that was necessary after hurricanes Harvey, Sandy, and Katrina and the building of cities that in future will be far more resilient in the face of storms. Right now, we are seeing an increase in the frequency and severity of storms that is almost indisputably a result of climate change. In this context it is completely understandable that mayors, faced with the significant financial and human cost of these storms, would support initiatives to mitigate greenhouse gas emissions in order to address the underlying causes that are so seriously impacting their cities.

Cities in different countries, provinces, and states have different powers and abilities, but mayors have one thing in common: the history and expectation of action. City governments tend to be less driven by ideological differences and are more practical: responsibilities such as overseeing new development, construction of parks, water and sewers, transportation, housing and other services for low-income residents all require that mayors act, and act in an effective way. While politicians from different political backgrounds might choose to address those challenges with different solutions, a mayor cannot simply pass legislation and then do nothing – residents of cities demand and expect real action.

This background has led to cities being unique incubators of interesting ideas and actions on climate change. At this moment in the world's history this catalog of actions is critical. It is clear that the measures taken to date by national governments are insufficient to meet the collective challenge of climate change. Indeed, some reports suggest that the current levels of action by governments will lead to a four-degree temperature rise by the end of this century, with resulting disastrous changes to the global climate and serious impact on human life, the forced resettlement of tens of millions of people due to desertification and crop loss, the necessity to rebuild cities to deal with sea-level rise and the increasing severity and frequency of storms, not to mention significant impact on nature.

If we are to build on the accord reached in Paris and hold global average temperature rise to 1.5 degrees, it is critical that we start today. And this is where the leadership of global mayors and cities matters the most. Because if we are to solve climate change, we need to start making changes now. The actions of the leadership of the world's great cities show us how.

Lowering Emissions through Clean Energy, Buildings, Transport, and Waste

Studies by the C40 Cities Climate Leadership Group have shown that about 70 per cent of the world's greenhouse gas emissions can be attributed to cities, predominately in four areas: the generation of electricity, the heating and cooling of buildings, transportation, and solid waste. The good news is that in each of these areas actions are taking place today that are making a dramatic difference in local greenhouse gas emissions, and taken together these actions can make a very real difference globally. The bad news is that these initiatives have not yet spread at the pace and scale needed.

It's the thesis of this book that by replicating the best and most effective ideas already implemented in at least one city, and by doing so at scale and pace internationally, we can make a significant leap forward in mitigating greenhouse gas emissions and put the world on a path to 1.5 degrees. None of the ideas discussed in this book require radical new technologies that are yet to be invented. All have been implemented somewhere and, if implemented broadly across a significant number of cities, will help to dramatically reduce greenhouse gas emissions. For me, this is an exciting prospect and gives hope that we can collectively address this unique challenge.

The book answers the question "What do cities need to do?" The first requirement is to have a plan, and Chapter 1 will discuss examples of the best city plans, what they do, and how they came about. In Los Angeles, Mayor Garcetti's bold Green New Deal plan starts with the five zeroes – a zero-emission power grid; zero-emission buildings and transport; zero waste and zero waste of water. It starts aggressively now, with longer-term goals for the most complicated challenges. All of the plans we see address the four areas mentioned above – how we generate our electricity, how we can heat and cool our buildings efficiently, transportation, and how we manage our waste – and try to do so in a way that is fair to the least well off in each city. Leaders include New York City, with its aggressive law mandating the reduction of carbon in existing buildings (and creating job-training programs for the boom in retrofitting work that will follow), and Shenzhen, China, where all transit vehicles and all taxis are powered by electricity – today. There are examples from the developing world too – such as how Accra, Ghana, has dealt with emissions from waste in a way that addresses public health and the environment, and that also works for the most disadvantaged in their society.

By addressing each of these areas with bold policies, leading cities are making significant progress. At least thirty-five cities can now say they have peaked emissions, and it is estimated that at least fifty major global cities will have climate plans consistent with the goals of the Paris Accord by the end of this year or early 2021. Unlike national governments, cities don't just talk – they act.

I believe there is significant potential to achieve exactly what is set out in this book because it is logical, affordable, and real. Most of all, it will be achieved because what each of these mayors has in common is that their actions to reduce greenhouse gas emissions are helping their cities be better, more interesting, more economically successful, and more socially equitable places to live. Mayors are elected to achieve these goals in cities around the world. I'm optimistic we will see these actions happen, both because they are possible and because voters will continue to support mayors who want to create those kinds of livable, prosperous, and inclusive cities.

I've had a unique opportunity to be inspired by this global leadership of my fellow mayors for nearly two decades. My wish is that readers will be equally inspired.

Chapter 1

Plans

"With flames on our hillsides and floods in our streets, cities cannot wait another moment to confront the climate crisis with everything we've got. LA is leading the charge, with a clear vision for protecting the environment and making our economy work for everyone."

With these words, Mayor Eric Garcetti unveiled Los Angeles' Green New Deal on April 28, 2019, a substantial augmentation of the city's 2015 Sustainable City Plan, reflecting current research that shows the need for more aggressive action to address the climate crisis.

From phasing out Styrofoam and single-use plastics to requiring buildings to become emissions free to saving an anticipated US$16 billion in health care expenses every year by 2050, LA's ambitious blueprint demonstrates how clear-sighted and equitable planning is allowing cities to drive the climate agenda forward, far more effectively than any other order of government.

***

Los Angeles.

Hollywood. Beaches. The Lakers of the National Basketball Association. Rolling hills. Traffic. And ... smog.

To those who grew up in the '60s, '70s, and '80s, that's the enduring image of Los Angeles – traffic, and smog, beneath the larger-than-life Hollywood sign. Los Angeles sits in a bowl surrounded by a series of beautiful hills and mountains. It's a heavily industrial city, and of course one with significant traffic challenges. According to reports, the air quality was so bad during and after the Second World War that consideration was given to moving the airport so pilots could see; car drivers were forced to pull over because their eyes stung so badly they couldn't drive; and when people blew their noses, the mucus was black. On June 26, 1943, a wave of smog hit Los Angeles that was so severe that people could not see more than three blocks. Striking in midsummer, it left residents with serious stinging and burning sensations in their eyes and throats.

Frequent incidents like this led to a public reaction from local government – and eventually the state. Research work started by the County of Los Angeles, along with intense public interest, led within a few years to California legislation that permitted cities and counties to establish air-quality districts with significant powers to address the myriad causes of the disastrously dirty air – industry, backyard incineration, traffic, and many others. The City of Los Angeles and Los Angeles County created Air Quality Districts (now subsumed into the South Coast Air Quality Management District). At the time this was not easy politically; industry was bitterly opposed. Some in industry argued, for example, that the smog was caused naturally by ocean breezes bringing ozone to the city, kept in by the hills and mountains that surround Los Angeles. These theories were quickly disproven by science, which showed that an array of sources – industry, traffic, natural forces, actions by individual households – all contributed to the terrible air. This knowledge boosted a strong public campaign that led to virtually unanimous passage of the necessary legislation by the state in 1947.

These efforts were followed over time by a wide variety of measures to address air-quality challenges. While air quality even today

September 15, 1955: After several motorcycle couriers from the Rapid Blueprint Company in Los Angeles became ill from the effects of smog, the owners issued gas masks to protect workers from poor air quality. Source: Bettmann/ Contributor.

is not pristine, it is vastly better than seventy years ago, when the issue was first addressed by local and state governments. The efforts have left legacies beyond environmental improvement – for example, the knowledge that collective action to address an environmental challenge is both possible and successful. But it needs collective will – and a plan. Action to stop air pollution in southern California has shown residents and elected officials what is possible. On air. On water. And now, on climate.

Committed City Leadership

During an extraordinary two weeks in late April 2019, Los Angeles, New York, and Vancouver all launched climate plans whose ambition matched the requirements of science – to peak emissions by 2020 and work toward carbon neutrality by 2050. In content, these plans were about much more than just climate mitigation: both

New York and Los Angeles named their plans Green New Deals in recognition that climate change is inherently unjust and that issues of equity and inclusion must be addressed by the plan if it is to succeed. Vancouver's plan was in response to a declaration of a climate emergency by its city council. Each addressed emissions from energy, buildings, transportation, and waste, and each also addressed the fundamental inequity involved in climate change – caused by the wealthy few, its impacts are felt first by the poorest in a city, then globally. Each of these bold plans sought to ensure that the least well off in their communities would benefit from the efforts to mitigate greenhouse gas emissions.

In Los Angeles, which owns the electric utility (the Los Angeles Department of Water and Power or LADWP), the plan focused first on generating zero-emission electricity by closing the remaining natural gas plants in Los Angeles and replacing them with clean energy. It then outlines a move to electric transport and electric heating and cooling of buildings using the clean grid – and has strong measures to move toward zero waste and zero waste of water.

New York analyzed its emissions and identified buildings as its priority, implementing a plan with mandatory measures for the reduction of carbon emissions in large buildings. Vancouver, in a Canadian province with a clean-energy grid, built on this strength with measures to promote a city where it is possible to live well without owning a car by supporting new public transport, walking, and cycling, and has ground-breaking legislation to dramatically reduce the carbon emissions of new buildings.

Why Plans?

To successfully mitigate emissions, the need for a climate plan is both obvious and subtle. As we have seen, planning is an integral part of the role of city governments. Mayors understand the strategic importance of plans, and complex organizations such as the civil service of a large city operate based on the instructions in city plans. Those instructions are even more essential for an issue such as climate change; that is, complex problems whose resolutions require coordinated action by many city departments and agencies – who might see climate action as outside their responsibility.

When I was still in office as mayor of Toronto, we instituted a program as part of our climate plan to encourage the installation of solar thermal hot-water heaters, which, on a south-facing roof, work surprisingly well in our climate. The program was part of a suite of measures adopted by city council to reduce the consumption of fossil fuels at the household level, and the heaters used sunlight to warm water for household use, displacing the natural-gas water heaters most common here. At the program launch at a house in the east end of Toronto, just before we took questions from the dozens of reporters and numerous television and radio stations, the local councilor leaned over to me and whispered in my ear, "I think you need to know, the plumbing department has refused to grant permits to solar hot-water heaters, including this one." It turned out that despite a bylaw from council authorizing the installation of solar thermal heating on single-family homes, the plumbing department took the view that until the bylaw governing its responsibilities also was changed it could not authorize the work! Fortunately no one in the press conference thought to ask if the installation had a plumbing permit.

A climate plan starts by measuring the amounts and sources of greenhouse gas in a city – known as an emissions inventory. It is critical to measure emissions so that the biggest sources can be addressed with accurate knowledge and steps to address them can be set out logically in a written document. But in a city-government context, the existence of a plan is equally important because it forces the system – the various departments and agencies – to act by incorporating climate actions into the everyday routine work. It is only in this way that a plan can be successfully implemented, and experience has shown that to mobilize these departments (who might not think climate change is their job), it is essential to prescribe goals for them and include them in the development of a plan. In this way, the plan gains from expert input – but also gains the confidence and personal commitment of those well beyond the city's environment department.

City governments are complicated organizations. They have jurisdiction over matters highly relevant to climate policy, such as parks and trees, buildings, transportation, roads, water, and wastewater. Historically and typically, these areas are administered by city departments heavily focused on those specific responsibilities. So, for example, the transportation department is typically focused on roads; a transit agency on transit; and the finance department on budget and financial oversight. Environmental matters, especially climate change, tend to cross all departments. To take advantage of opportunities and be successful in mobilizing the significant city resources in the same direction, it's necessary to have a plan that everyone is obliged to follow.

What Do Plans Need to Do?

In 2015, the C40 Cities Climate Leadership Group and Arup engineers asked the question "What needs to be done by the largest cities in order to do their share to help the world avoid dangerous climate change?" In climate shorthand, this is known as a "1.5 degree" world – which means holding overall global average temperature to an increase of no more than 1.5 degrees. This is now generally accepted as necessary to avoid the most catastrophic elements of climate change and is highlighted by the science underlying the latest reports by the Intergovernmental Panel on Climate Change (and even those issued by the White House).

The Arup research showed that to do their share, cities in the developed world needed to peak their emissions by 2020, more or less halve them by 2030, on a trajectory to carbon neutrality by 2050. (The peak could be a little later in the developing world but the trajectory has to be the same.) The C40 calls this Deadline 2020 (D2020), and so far more than one hundred major global cities have announced that they will produce D2020-compliant plans.

One of the important strategies used by mayors to address climate change is international collaboration. The C40 Cities Climate Leadership Group, of which I was chair from 2008 to 2010, was started by London mayor Ken Livingstone in 2005. Mayor Livingstone saw that the world was not acting quickly enough on climate change and believed that the voices of the mayors of the world's major cities could, in a significant and positive way, affect international action on climate. In addition, their actions, when multiplied at scale, could meaningfully reduce global emissions. Today, the C40 has ninety-four members, who represent city-regions with more than 750 million people, a huge portion of the world's greenhouse gas emissions, and 25 per cent of the world's economy. Their actions have global implications.

Since inception, the organization has been enormously influential and has placed cities squarely at the heart of international conversations on climate. The actions by its members – global cities such as Johannesburg, Tokyo, Cape Town, London, Beijing, Rio, and Paris – collectively are making a difference to climate already, and the best of these actions, if undertaken globally at scale, will make an immediate and lasting major difference. The current chair is Mayor Eric Garcetti of Los Angeles, a recognized climate leader in his own right.

Importantly, these cities have shown that city plans can work. The most successful have shown that it is possible to achieve dramatic carbon reductions while enhancing the life of residents of the city and helping the city to prosper. In fact, in almost every case, strong climate plans are being made and implemented simultaneously with strong economic prosperity in these cities.

Do City Plans Make a Difference?

Can the world's major cities save the planet entirely on their own? Perhaps not – although, as stated in the preface, C40's studies show that about 70 per cent of the world's greenhouse gas emissions can be attributed to cities, generally in the areas of waste management, transportation, buildings, and electricity generation. (These figures are known as scope-two emissions; that is, emissions accounted for by city activities even if they don't occur physically within the city.

For example, the greenhouse gas emissions of a coal-fired electricity plant to supply electricity to a city would be included in this measure, even if the plant were located outside the city boundaries.)

Further studies have demonstrated where cities need to focus. Both the Coalition for Urban Transitions' report, released in September 2019, and the McKinsey Center for Business and the Environment's *Focused Acceleration* report (2017) clearly demonstrate that city leadership can make huge advances if city actions focus on those priorities of electricity, buildings, transportation, and waste management. Figure 1.1 is a chart from McKinsey that measures the most significant outcomes and their likely impacts. The ranges depend on city types as defined in the report (i.e., dense like New York, spread out like Houston, dense like a major city in the developing world, etc.).

Will these plans work? The answer is a resounding yes. Good examples can come from my home city of Toronto as well as Oslo in Norway. Both cities are in oil-producing countries. Toronto is Canada's biggest city with a heavy industrial heritage (albeit a city where much of the manufacturing base has moved to the suburbs, the United States, Mexico, or China). The city remains the economic heart of Canada, being home to five of the six major banks, head offices of most insurance companies and investment houses, significant information-technology companies, film, television and media companies, and construction and development companies, and is still home to a significant food-manufacturing sector.

Proven Effective: Toronto's "Change Is in the Air"

Toronto's path to dramatic reductions in greenhouse gas emissions demonstrates what is possible and can be undertaken by any large city. What did Toronto do? Conceptually, it was simple. It set greenhouse gas reduction targets based on the Kyoto Protocol, measured Toronto's sources of emissions, and developed a plan to address those sources. The plan required re-evaluation over time, thereby providing an opportunity to assess both progress and the

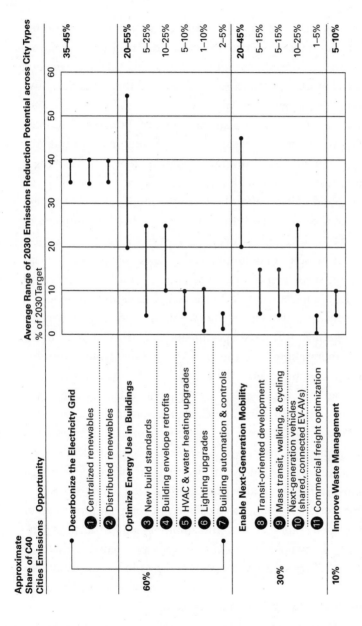

Figure 1.1: Effectiveness of City Actions

This figure demonstrates the effectiveness of city actions in reducing greenhouse gases when focus is placed on electricity, buildings, transportation, and waste management. Source: Exhibit from A Strategic Approach to Climate Action in Cities – Focused Acceleration, November 2017, state of scientific knowledge about climate change. The first plan, "Change Is in the Air," was adopted unanimously by Toronto city council in 2007.

It's important to understand the elements that allowed Toronto to pass an ambitious climate strategy. First of all was a strong political culture. Toronto has a history of action on environmental matters, and residents both expect and demand that their city councilors and mayor show leadership.

But success in getting a plan through city council and adopted as legislation is only the first step. Toronto's work in developing the plan shows that there are several important steps to developing a strong and resilient plan with a good likelihood of success. First, there was good collaboration between the political arm, through the office of the mayor, and the civil service in the development of the plan. Second, the plan covered a significant range of actions, very few of which could dramatically decrease greenhouse gas emissions on their own but taken together could have a powerful impact. Third, the plan had clear targets and goals and was based on a comprehensive emissions inventory. Finally, the plan consciously brought together different departments and areas of the city to ensure collaboration in both the plan's development and delivery.

The plan contained more than 120 actions in the areas of transportation, buildings, and waste management. It engaged residents and built on partnerships with public and private institutions. It was helped by the provincial government's closure of the Lakeview coal-fired power plant in 2005, which, while located outside Toronto, supplied significant amounts of electricity to the city – which resulted in a significant and permanent reduction of emissions.

While not all the actions envisioned in the plan proceeded at the scale hoped – for example, the ambitious rapid transit expansion strategy known as Transit City has not proceeded at the pace expected – the city achieved its goals and had reduced greenhouse gas emissions in the Toronto geographic area by 15 per cent by 2012, as demonstrated by an external evaluation. A second evaluation, using 2017 data and reported in 2018, showed that Toronto is now 33 per cent below 1990 levels of greenhouse gas emissions, and a

TOTAL GREENHOUSE GAS EMISSIONS

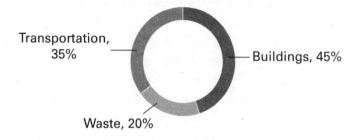

Transportation, 35%

Buildings, 45%

Waste, 20%

BUILDINGS

Electricity, 12%

Natural Gas, 88%

WASTE

Waste Transport, 1%

Landfill, 99%

TRANSPORTATION

Cars, 39%

SUVs, Vans, Light Trucks, 41%

Heavy Vehicles, 20%

Figure 1.2: Toronto's Greenhouse Gas Emissions, 2016
The major sources of greenhouse gas emissions in Toronto match those of most cities, which collectively account for 70 per cent of worldwide emissions. Source: Based on data from City of Toronto, Transform T.O. Report 1: Short-Term Strategies, 2016, *November 2016.*

new plan was adopted by council to strengthen progress. The 2016 emissions are shown in Figure 1.2.

A typical criticism from those seeking to thwart climate action is that taking such action hurts the economy. This is a false argument: the real costs of climate change are the costs of inaction (for instance, the billions in damage caused by the increasing frequency and severity of storms are real and result in substantial costs to governments, insurers, people, and business). The economy of Toronto proves the point. Since the passage in 2007 of its first climate plan, employment in the city of Toronto has increased significantly: according to the Conference Board of Canada, growth in Toronto has considerably exceeded national averages at least since 2009. The average house price nearly doubled between

2007 and 2017 (in fact, like many other North American cities, the challenge facing Toronto has been one of affordability due to increased housing costs.)

I am not arguing that the city's efforts to address climate change have directly caused the strong economic activity, as I have not seen a study that validates that point. However, it is clear from the Toronto example that strong action to reduce greenhouse gas emissions does not inhibit economic prosperity as argued by leading figures from conservative political movements and some parts of the fossil fuel industry. Such an argument does not stand up to any scrutiny whatsoever.

The Next Frontier: Oslo and City-Based Carbon Budgets

While Toronto remains an excellent example of leadership in the North American context, Oslo, the capital of Norway, has gone even further. In addition to developing an emissions inventory (see Figure 1.3), a plan, and actions to address greenhouse gas emissions, Oslo has also introduced a carbon budget.

The Oslo carbon budget is fascinating and is the world's leading example of how to integrate greenhouse gas emission reduction into the basics of government planning.

Oslo has ambitious goals for carbon reduction:

- 36 per cent below 1990 levels by 2020
- 50 per cent below by 2022
- 95 per cent below by 2030

Electricity is currently 98 per cent from hydro – which means that the electrification of heating and transportation is clean and likely to reduce greenhouse gas emissions significantly.

Oslo's climate budget is treated as a part of the city budget and is passed as a chapter in that budget with a debate and vote by city council. The budget is adopted annually and is managed by

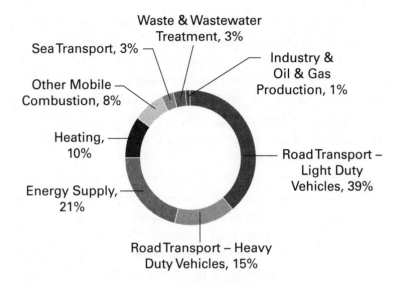

Figure 1.3: Oslo's Greenhouse Gas Emissions, 2016
Oslo's implementation of a carbon budget allows it to address greenhouse gas emissions from all sectors as a primary element of planning. Source: Based on data from Norwegian Environment Agency, 2018.

the finance department, a subtle but important matter. It may not be obvious that the finance department should be responsible for greenhouse gas emissions, but this administrative detail is of critical importance. Finance touches all city departments, and there are recognized approval and administrative structures overseen by finance for the financial budget that can be adopted for a carbon budget. City departments are familiar with these approval processes, which means a direct operational integration of climate and energy strategy into the city's administrative operations – and recognized accountability measures.

All city departments are responsible for proposing measures and for implementing the actions. For each measure and action, the designated responsible department or agency must track and report on progress three times annually so changes can be undertaken if required. Importantly, council has directed that the city cannot generate more CO_2 than budgeted – period.

As it is not always possible to precisely measure emissions as they occur – to give a simple example, live monitoring of vehicle exhaust does not exist – simple and reliable indicators are used by city departments. In this example, the number of vehicles passing through toll gates or the rate of e-vehicle adoption would be used to create data sufficient to judge whether emissions from transportation would increase or decrease as a result of a proposed measure's implementation.

The most significant factor, though, is not in these implementation details – effective as they are – but in the fact of the carbon budget itself. A city department cannot undertake a project without considering greenhouse gases in the same way that the department cannot undertake a project without considering the necessary financial resources. If the recreation department wanted to build a new curling rink for a community center, it would need to consider energy sources, insulation, and so on in the same way it would have traditionally considered cost. This remarkable and simple mechanism forces a department to directly address its environmental footprint – analogous to the existence of a plan forcing the department to consider that issue as part of its operations, but more directly effective because it is mandated. And that mandate has direct impacts in the critical areas for Oslo of buildings, transportation, and waste management.

Oslo performs one other action extremely well as part of its climate plan: storytelling. Oslo tells positive stories of how people live better lives with climate action in order to promote even greater action. It avoids negative messaging and focuses on changing behavior rather than attitudes. The Oslo website regularly features stories about climate actions – for example, "We haven't regretted even for one second switching to an electric van" or "It's great that this electric bus is so quiet to drive." The city provides educational material for schools and has developed the Oslo Centre for Urban Ecology to engage citizens in ecological work in the city, encourage local environmental and climate measures, and "help the city's residents to feel a sense of ownership over, and see the potential in, the shift toward becoming a zero-emissions society."

Making Plans Equitable and Fair: Inclusive Climate Action

This book argues that actions in leading cities to dramatically reduce greenhouse gas emissions in the areas of energy, buildings, transportation, and waste have the potential to help the world solve the climate crisis. By replicating these actions at scale – for example, all cities mandating electric taxis, such as Shenzhen, China, has – greenhouse gas emissions globally can be dramatically reduced, and the city involved can become a better place to live. By demonstrating that climate action works, city leadership can overcome the biggest challenges to solving the climate crisis: inertia and the perception that measures to address climate change make people's lives more expensive, more difficult, or worse.

One of the advantages of city governments in almost every country is that they have a strong connection with their residents: the responsibilities of city governments require direct connection to residents, as city councilors typically have much smaller districts than regional or national politicians, and residents identify strongly with where they live. Consequently, this has tended to mean that cities have developed a strength in public engagement – and a resulting strength in public trust.

In the context of climate, this trust is significant as it is a critical asset for cities and their mayors in leading change. At the same time, the strong connections to residents ensure that cities often recognize issues well before national governments do. As a result, mayors increasingly are seeing the connection between equity – inclusivity – and their political ability to act on climate.

Climate change is unfair. The majority of the world's greenhouse gas emissions have been caused in support of the lives of the most well off, but its impact tends to be felt most by the least well off, both globally and within particular cities. Fairness requires that the needs of the least well off be made a priority when addressing climate change, and politics requires the same. The inherent inequity in the impact of climate change has the potential to derail efforts to reduce greenhouse gas emissions unless the needs of the most vulnerable are included in the climate plan and the residents themselves included in the planning.

A number of global cities have prioritized inclusivity in their climate plans and have created pilot projects. While solutions are not so easily transferable from city to city as many other climate actions, the underlying principles are clear: include low-income people in your climate planning, then listen to and act on their needs. Address air quality, health, and other issues at the same time as reducing greenhouse gases. Create jobs and opportunity. Make living less expensive and the quality of life better for the least well off.

In the same way that climate actions can spread from city to city, these good ideas can as well. For example, inclusion of process is a principle that all cities can follow – perhaps in different ways, but the underlying principle is the same. Paris and Barcelona are examples of what is possible when engaging residents in climate planning, listening to their concerns, and acting.

On the Climate Front Lines

Rio de Janeiro is a fascinating and historic city, with legendary beaches and a vibrant cultural life. It is also the home of advanced thinking about how to create a city that is not only sustainable environmentally but also socially.

Under former mayor Eduardo Paes, Rio advanced its climate agenda strongly, aligning its plans to the ambitions of the Paris Accord and identifying a path to carbon neutrality by 2050. At the same time, recognizing the need for social and economic development for the least well off in Rio, the city signed the 2030 agenda for social development, thereby making a formal commitment to honor and achieve the United Nations' sustainable development goals (SDGs).

Rio's insight was to combine its work on the SDGs with its climate-action plan, starting by including affected citizens in the development of the plan. In this way not only could Rio build public support for the plans, it could also ensure that they were developed in a way that truly meets the needs of residents in an inclusive and just manner.

"Today, cities and nations alike have the opportunity to build on the momentum created in Paris. We have the opportunity to put the world on a low-carbon pathway. Let us seize it."

– Mayor Eduardo Paes (Rio), April 2016

Participatory Budgets in Paris

In 2014 Paris began a process of participatory budgeting. Participatory budgeting means giving residents the right to make some (or all) of the decisions about spending priorities for a city government. The city committed to setting aside €500 million, or about 5 per cent of its total spending, for allocation through participatory budgeting between 2014 and 2020. The city has specified that at least 20 per cent of these funds should address climate issues. This participatory budgeting process has engaged nearly 200,000 residents, with the intention of building a stronger relationship between city hall and residents – and with the potential of meeting the needs of residents as expressed by them.

Building on its experience in participatory budgeting, Paris listened to the needs that residents expressed. In its approach to climate planning Paris put its focus on fuel poverty (defined as households that spent more than 10 per cent of their income on heating and cooling residences), which it sought to address by a combination of subsidies, energy retrofits, and assistance to residents in learning how to better manage home energy consumption.

Accordingly, Paris has an extensive program of energy retrofits in its publicly owned housing. Building on this program, Paris made alleviating fuel poverty a specific goal of the climate-action plan, with the objective of undertaking energy retrofits on five thousand apartments annually. As a result, Paris has already seen a reduction in the energy demand in these buildings and a significant decrease in the number of residents seeking subsidies – making residents economically better off and addressing the sources of greenhouse gases at the same time.

On the Climate Front Lines

New York City has addressed the issue of equitable employment directly as it builds meaningful plans to address climate change. It has recognized that cities must seize the opportunity to engage people from low-income communities in the new jobs and opportunities that come from climate action. On April 22, 2017, Earth Day, Mayor Bill de Blasio and the Building and Construction Trades Council announced a pre-apprenticeship program designed to train people for well-paid work in the construction sector. These opportunities were among three thousand created by the NYC Green Jobs Corps program and were designed to help fill employment opportunities created by the city's ambitious energy retrofit goals for the city's public and private buildings. The NYC Green Jobs Corps was modeled after a successful job-training program post Hurricane Sandy ("Build It Back"), in which more than 20 per cent of workers lived in areas impacted by the hurricane.

Environmental Justice in Barcelona

Barcelona expressed similar principles in the development of its climate plan. Its 2018 climate plan had an environmental justice and "citizen co-production" focus, allowing the plan to address economic and social inequality at the same time as it addressed climate mitigation and adaptation. To successfully undertake such measures, Barcelona recognized that it was essential to engage the residents of low-income neighborhoods and others vulnerable to the impacts of climate change in the plan's development. This engagement provides city authorities with a greater understanding of the needs of the most vulnerable and the potential solutions – and with a chance to demonstrate that people have a real say over the decisions that affect their lives.

Barcelona built an extensive community-engagement process that deliberately reached beyond those who might normally be engaged in an environmental consultation. The city worked closely with those who already were working with low-income neighborhoods or with other vulnerable groups, such as nongovernmental organizations, social associations, and private businesses. The city recognized an important fact that would be true in most places – those most affected by climate change might well not be those who participate in public discussions. Low-income residents of a city, by definition, tend to be both excluded from power and the manifestations of power – such as direct engagement with government – and preoccupied with ensuring their own economic survival. In this context, special efforts must be made to connect with low-income and other disempowered residents; otherwise, their voices will not be part of the conversation, and any solutions developed will likely not meet their needs.

Accordingly, Barcelona ran a lengthy (six months) process in 2017 to engage representatives from partner organizations and residents at an early stage of the climate-planning process and followed up with a presentation of the plan in February 2018. Barcelona has reported that 85 per cent of the recommendations received during this process were incorporated into the plan – demonstrating to those affected and participating that their voices mattered and strengthening the plan by virtue of the recommendations.

Barcelona's climate plan explicitly addresses equity issues and can be a model for others. Previous work by the city, such as the 2016 health survey, had demonstrated significant connections between the impact of climate change and poverty – ranging from issues such as energy poverty to the differential effects of heat and rising temperatures on the elderly, the young, and women. As a result, Barcelona's climate plan included a series of actions that would particularly benefit the most vulnerable residents. Consistent with many other cities, Barcelona's climate plan is well organized thematically and consists of very specific actions grouped into thematic areas: 1) people first, 2) starting at home, 3) transforming communal spaces, 4) climate economy, and 5) building together. The plan is structured with "plans of action" according to the themes and then more than two hundred specific actions. For instance, the theme of "people first" has plans of action for improving and adapting services, facilities, and homes for the most vulnerable; for preventing gas, water, or electricity from being cut off; and for preventing harm from excessive heat.

Barcelona detailed at the outset quite specific actions to achieve these goals. For example, as part of the "preventing excessive heat" plan, the city's goal is to ensure that all of the population is within a ten-minute walk of a climate shelter by 2030. Consequently, the city is mapping all potential places where people could find refuge – from libraries to air-conditioned malls, to parks with significant shade cover – and considering issues such as availability at different times of the day, physical accessibility, etc. This information will be used to identify gaps in available facilities and decide where new facilities might be created.

More famous are the Barcelona "superblocks" – an urban-planning idea that has changed the way districts are organized. Barcelona has prioritized the movement of people over vehicles by making local streets in a neighborhood – or superblock – virtually car free (local traffic only), while enhancing amenities for pedestrians – such as tree cover and benches. While controversial at inception, the superblocks have proven popular since implemented, as they have improved local quality of life, personal mobility, air quality – and local economic activity. While the original superblock plan lowers emissions from automobile traffic, Barcelona has used the concept of superblocks in its climate plan to help build social resilience as well.

The city has organized home-care social workers on a similar (but not necessarily identical) basis to assist dependent residents – such as the elderly – by ensuring that the same social workers regularly visit and become part of the trusted fabric of the neighborhood. These workers will be available to assist with climate matters – such as reducing energy expenditure and coping with extreme heat events – as well as more traditional forms of assistance, all the while supporting the building of a sense of community and social cohesion.

Starting with an inclusive process is critical: if low-income and other marginalized residents are not heard from directly, it is far less likely that a climate plan will address their needs. As we have seen from both Barcelona and Paris, an inclusive process can help lead to inclusive outcomes. These can move far beyond energy issues: economic security and health impacts of poor environmental conditions are both issues raised during public outreach. And cities are addressing these issues – systematically and effectively.

> *"We are disconnecting the oligopolies and connecting to renewables, to self-sufficiency and energy control."*
>
> **– Mayor Ada Colau (Barcelona), May 2019**

The Final Word

The best city climate plans reduce greenhouse gas emissions effectively, in line with scientific requirements to hold overall temperature rise to 1.5 degrees. The best climate plans also do something else: they address issues of prosperity, health, and inclusion, thereby putting cities in a unique position to deliver on both meaningful climate action and social justice.

Chapter 2

Energy and Electricity

EnWave Corporation is a private company that owns a large steam-heating district energy system in downtown Toronto and an equally large district cooling system. It is a successor to the Toronto District Heating Corporation (TDHC), the city-owned utility that supplied highly efficient district heat to public buildings in Toronto starting in 1980. At that time the steam-heating subsidiary of Toronto Hydro (owned by the city) merged with the Toronto Hospitals Steam Corporation to become TDHC. It later built the first large-scale municipal district cooling project in the world, which opened on August 17, 2004. The idea for the district cooling came from the brilliant engineer Robert Tamblyn, who reportedly got the idea for district cooling when he was working at the T. Eaton department store in the 1940s. At the time, the company used fans to blow air across the cold-water pipes to cool the women's nightwear section. Mr. Tamblyn's insight and brilliant engineering eventually led to the use of cold lake water to cool most buildings in downtown Toronto using less than a tenth of the energy required by traditional cooling systems. On October 4, 2012, Mr. Tamblyn died at age ninety-one. In a very odd coincidence, on the same day, legal approval was given for EnWave to be privatized by the City of Toronto and sold to Brookfield Asset Management.

***

On a cold winter's day in Toronto, Canada, the air will be remarkably clear, and the sky brilliant blue. The sun will sparkle off Lake Ontario, and if there has been a recent snowfall, the snow will glisten. There might be a little ice on Lake Ontario pushed to the shore by the action of the waves. The peaks and troughs are highlighted by the low angle of the sun.

From Exhibition Place, adjacent to the shore of Lake Ontario, on such a day you might be able to see the mist of Niagara Falls hanging in the sky, more than forty miles away across the lake. In the foreground, you will see a 299-foot-tall cream-colored wind turbine, standing high into the sky, and you might possibly hear a slight hum. Installed in 2002 by the Toronto Renewable Energy Collective, the turbine was the first within the urban boundaries of a major North American city. It's a highly visible demonstration of Toronto's commitment to sustainable innovation.

Each year, Exhibition Place attracts more than 5.5 million visitors to its trade and consumer shows, the popular and highly successful local soccer team Toronto FC, and the Canadian National Exhibition. All the visitors will see the wind turbine, but what they do not see is equally as impressive. On the flat rooftops of some of the industrial buildings that are lined up on the north side of the exhibition grounds are two giant solar arrays. Hundreds and hundreds of solar panels silently, quietly, and efficiently generating electricity. At installation, both of them could claim to be the largest urban solar array in Canada. As well, there is a highly efficient trigenerator on site – meaning that Toronto's historic exhibition grounds generate as much electricity on site as they consume, despite being busy with multitudes of energy-intensive events virtually every day of the week, year round.

The WindShare ExPlace Turbine. Owned by the Toronto Renewable Energy Co-Operative (Windshare), the project was built to demonstrate the viability of a wind turbine in an urban setting. It generates from 600 to 625 kilowatts or about enough power for a neighborhood. Source: NicolasMcComber/iStockphoto.com.

Clean Electricity Is Critical to Climate Action

Exhibition Place is a showcase of what creative city leadership can do to address the critical issue of greenhouse gas emissions from the generation of electricity. It is well established that how we generate electricity has significant consequences for climate change. Coal, for example, when used as the fuel for electric power plants generates substantial carbon dioxide (the most significant greenhouse gas), as well as nitrogen oxide, mercury, dioxides, and other serious air pollutants.

The figures used in this book for estimates of greenhouse gas emissions by cities will typically count emissions from electricity generation, including those from a plant that supplies a city, even if it is outside that city. At the same time, cities' regulatory authority over or ownership of electric utilities varies significantly. In some jurisdictions such as Texas and California, cities will own the utility that generates electricity; in others such as Ontario, they will own the distribution utility; and in still others they will have no direct authority but will have considerable influence. Whatever the legal role, cities have recognized how critical it is to move rapidly to clean sources of electricity and are taking serious measures to do exactly that. The role of mayors in advocating for a broader energy transition – closing coal- and gas-fired power plants, for example – is important, as are the creative actions of those mayors in finding other ways to unlock and expedite a transition to clean energy.

This chapter will explore examples of effective leadership from cities that have significantly decarbonized their electricity – starting with those that do own their utilities.

Municipally Owned Utilities: The Emergence of Distributed Energy

Historically, electricity has been usually generated by large power plants, and the electricity distributed by power lines over long distances to those who use it, with the possible exception of certain power plants designed to support particular industrial operations. This traditional model of generating and transmitting electricity is known as a "grid," but conceptually it is being challenged by modern technologies. It is now possible to think of electric power as something being potentially generated in small amounts at a household level, with any excess being sold back into the grid for consumption by others. (Germany is the best-known example of this new approach, which is called distributed energy.) Solar power – fueled by sunlight – is an example of a renewable source of energy that can be successful in many places today, at a very low cost. Unlike fossil fuels, solar is clean – and does not run out. Essentially, solar photovoltaics (known as PVs) turn sunshine directly into electricity through solar cells made of silicon wafers that are assembled into the solar panels we see, which generate direct current (like batteries). If used at a household level, the electricity generated is fed into the electrical panel through an inverter that changes the electricity from direct current to alternating for use in the house or in appliances.

Austin Energy: Bold Leadership from the City that Proudly "Keeps It Weird"

Austin, Texas, is hot in the summer. Very hot. Over the past twenty years, it has been having on average more than thirty days of temperatures above 38°C (100°F) per year, and that average is rising, likely due to the impact of climate change. That weather means more demand for air conditioning, which uses more electricity, which generates greenhouse gases, which cause global warming, which causes extreme heat days in Austin. It is a vicious cycle, one that Austin is working hard to change. In 2007 Austin City Council resolved to "make Austin the leading city in the nation in the effort to reduce the negative impacts of global warming," setting a goal of reducing greenhouse gas emissions to 20 per cent below 2005 levels by 2020 and being net zero by 2050. (Net zero means if there are any greenhouse gas emissions greater than zero, they will be captured or offset; for example, by sequestering in concrete or by planting trees, both of which remove carbon from the atmosphere.)

The electric utility in Austin (Austin Energy) is municipally owned, and the city has worked with Austin Energy to make significant progress on its climate goals. (There are two or three other smaller utilities in the county, including that of the University of Texas. They have cooperated with the city as well.) In addition to environmental constraints, Austin has had a significant period of population growth and regulatory constraints over the price of electricity. Electricity prices cannot rise by more than an average of

2 per cent per year, and overall rates must remain below the fiftieth percentile for the state of Texas.

The approach of the city and its utility to these challenges has been highly effective. It involves a combination of reducing demand through conservation, investment in energy-storage solutions, peak-demand management, and investment in local solar projects. In 1982, Austin Energy began to build what it calls a "Conservation Energy Plant." Rather than build a new power plant to supply growing demand for electricity, Austin developed conservation programs to offset that growing demand and eliminate the need to build new capacity. The program focused on the energy efficiency of buildings and electrical equipment and it worked – the utility avoided building a new plant and saved significant costs while doing so.

That approach was so successful that Austin is creating its second Conservation Energy Plant. Electricity rates are used to help incentivize reduced use: rates increase step-wise with consumption. Peak-demand management involves a voluntary program for homes and businesses in which Austin Energy remotely controls the thermostats for limited times on peak-demand days. A district chilling system has also been developed whereby ice is made at night and the cool water is used to cool the buildings in the hot part of the day. Finally, Austin has invested heavily in local and utility-scale solar projects. In the city, you can subscribe for 100 per cent renewable energy, rebates are offered for solar installation, and higher rates are offered for locally generated solar.

Because a significant portion of Austin's greenhouse gas emissions comes from electricity use in the city, renewable sources of energy are a priority. The current energy supply is a mix of wind, natural gas, coal, nuclear, solar, and biomass. By 2022, the city plans to end the use of coal power, but a full switch away from fossil fuels requires an energy supply that is flexible, reliable, and predictable, and it also requires energy storage. These technologies are in development to support the expansion of renewable sources that are intermittent. Austin Energy is considering many possible approaches, from large battery storage to thermal storage, to compressed-air energy storage.

Austin Energy offers rebates to help reduce the cost of installing residential solar systems and pays residents for the electricity they generate. It says the most optimally positioned solar PV system faces due south and is tilted to a thirty-degree angle. If a south-facing roof is not available, west facing is generally the next best, and east-facing solar panels also work. Source: RoschetzkyIstockPhoto/iStockphoto.com.

"*As your mayor, I'm proud to have joined almost 400 other US mayors to adopt, honor and uphold the Paris Climate Agreement. I reiterated our commitment last October at the Paris Climate Conference and again in December when I signed the Chicago Climate Charter at the North American Climate Summit.*

Last year this Council, thanks to the leadership of CM Pool, upped our renewable energy goals from 55 per cent by 2025 – to 65 per cent by 2027 (and asked for a plan to get us up to 75 per cent). This is one of the most ambitious clean energy goals in the country.

And we're well on our way toward meeting that goal. We're beginning the process to close our only coal plant and increase our use of renewable clean power at Austin Energy.

Last year we bought more solar and wind to push us over 50 per cent renewables by 2020. The economics of such energy have gotten so competitive, that the last renewable energy contract signed by Austin Energy will serve to reduce the rate-payer cost."

– Mayor Steve Adler (Austin), State of the City address, 2018

In pursuit of these goals, the city has worked with Austin Energy to create an ambitious residential rooftop solar program. The program provides subsidies and incentives to residential homeowners to install rooftop solar, and the utility commits to buying excess electricity from the homes. Priced in a way that encourages homeowners to install the solar panels, the utility is still saving money over the cost of building a new power plant. Combined with industrial-scale solar installations and energy from wind, Austin Energy is confident of meeting its current target of 65 per cent generation by renewables by 2025.

The City of Austin has led the way in moving to renewable energy in its own operations. By 2012, municipal buildings were powered with 100 per cent renewable energy, and Austin was the first large municipality in the United States to reach this goal.

This municipal leadership is important. Although Austin is a progressive, modern city, with a world-stature university, a massive annual music and arts festival (SXSW – South by Southwest), and a wonderful slogan – "Keep It Weird" – it is still in the heart of Texas, the world capital of the oil industry. It would be difficult indeed to ask residents to adopt significant new technologies to move away from oil and gas if the city government itself could not point to its own success.

The plan is Austin is working. By 2018, 38 per cent of all electricity citywide was sourced from renewables and included more than eight thousand rooftop solar installations. This success has allowed Austin to think about doing even more, and it is in the midst of developing a new action agenda to do more faster, starting by reviewing the feasibility of shortening its timelines and increasing its targets.

On the Climate Front Lines

Cape Town is a beautiful ocean front city. It's also a city faced with extremes of wealth and poverty and with infrastructure challenges, such as frequent electricity brownouts and blackouts. South Africa is a country that primarily generates power from coal-fired power plants, despite favorable conditions for wind and solar. Eskom, the South African publicly owned utility, is approximately 90 per cent powered by coal, which contributes significantly to the country's greenhouse gas emissions. It also has significant political power and a regulatory environment that protects it. Despite this, Cape Town has taken strong steps to create a much cleaner electricity grid, provide reliable power, and create employment opportunities through its Small Scale Energy Generation Program — which promotes rooftop solar and small-scale wind projects. It has also created a program to train technicians that is heavily subsidized for men and free for women to ensure that low-income workers can have access to these jobs. Under the leadership of Mayor Patricia de Lille, the city also sued to establish the right for owners to sell electricity back to the grid — taking on a reluctant national government and utility.

"In government, things don't just happen by wishing ... later on, you find that people have now bought into the idea and understand the benefit of what we are achieving. Then it's much easier — you

have leadership at all levels bought into the new way of doing things."

– Mayor Patricia de Lille (Cape Town), 2017

Municipal Utilities: Los Angeles

Los Angeles is another powerful example of leadership by a city that owns its electric utility – in this case the Los Angeles Department of Water and Power.

The LA climate plan – LA's Green New Deal – aims to improve the lives of the residents of Los Angeles, particularly the most vulnerable citizens, while dramatically lowering greenhouse gas emissions. As a part of this strategy, the plan's goal is to use 100 per cent renewable energy by 2045. In the near term, the target is 55 per cent renewables by 2025. The plan has a three-pronged approach: progressively increase local solar, add energy storage, and use demand-response programs. The LADWP has pledged to end all fossil fuel generation by 2029 (except for an already underway project to convert to natural gas a coal-fired power plant owned by the LADWP but located in Utah). LA's sources of greenhouse gas emissions are set out in Figure 2.1.

LA has succeeded in shifting electricity to renewables from coal, as shown in Figure 2.2.

Los Angeles has very significant grid-scale solar today. (Grid scale in this context means a large power plant. In the case of solar it would typically mean a giant solar array located outside a city, often in a desert or other place with near-continuous sunshine.) Since 2013, LA typically has had the most solar capacity of any US city. Today, the equivalent of more than half a million homes could be powered with the power output of Los Angeles' wind and solar installations currently owned by the LADWP.

LA has also been making strides to enable significant solar installations within city boundaries by launching a feed-in-tariff

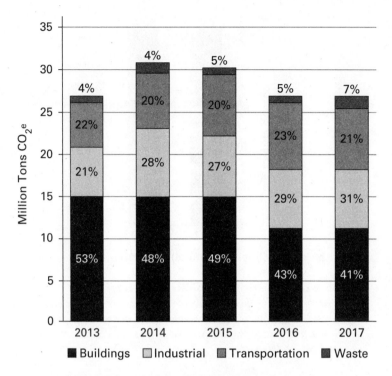

Figure 2.1: LA's Greenhouse Gas Emissions, 2013–2017
Emissions in the LA area are declining. With new action in the Green New Deal, they are set to decline much faster. Source: Based on data from City of Los Angeles, LA's Green New Deal: Sustainable City Plan 2019, *2019.*

(FiT) program in 2013. A feed-in-tariff is a way to pay people for electricity they generate, often but not exclusively at small scale (such as rooftop solar). It is an important step toward a program of distributed generation. When completed, LA's program will have enabled 150 megawatts of large solar installations on rooftops and vacant land in the city, about equivalent to the energy produced by one-fourth of a new natural gas power plant – significant indeed.

As part of a longer-term strategy, incentives were available between 1999 and 2018 to subsidize the purchase of solar panels, with greater subsidies available to governments, nonprofits, and affordable housing. That program has now been terminated because the dramatic reduction in the price of solar PV has meant that the

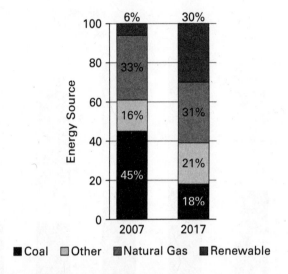

Figure 2.2: LA's Electricity Mix Shifts, 2007–2017
Los Angeles has started relying more on renewable energy to reduce dependency on coal–based energy. Source: Based on data from California Energy Commission, published in the Los Angeles Times, *"Los Angeles Is Finally Ditching Coal," 16 July 2019.*

incentives are no longer economically necessary. They were extremely effective: over twenty years they helped to create 268 megawatts of power from 34,440 installations.

LA recognizes the importance of equity when it comes to solar power – that the cost of electricity (and the economic benefits from a feed-in-tariff) should be shared by all residents. Accordingly, through the Solar Rooftops Program homeowners are able to lease their roof for the installation of solar panels, and the Shared Solar Program allows residents of multifamily dwellings to subscribe to offset portions of their energy use with solar energy every month at fixed prices for terms of up to ten years. Both programs are designed to allow underrepresented groups (such as low-income residents and renters) to participate in the solar market and benefit from solar savings.

The Green Power Program also allows participants to source all or a portion of their electricity from green power for a small increase in cost. By 2021, LA hopes to add energy storage to its FiT program, require all new parking structures to have solar panels, and launch a program to allow residents of multifamily buildings to share the economic benefits of solar installations on their buildings.

LA has significant plans for energy storage that focus on the development of a renewables hub in facilities owned by the LA Department of Water and Power in Utah. The LADWP currently owns a large share of a big coal-fired power plant (the Intermountain Plant) in Utah, as well as the transmission lines that bring the power to LA. Renovations are underway to retrofit that coal plant with natural gas, dramatically lowering emissions. At that site, there also is significant potential for grid-scale solar and wind, which could use the same transmission lines and lessen reliance on the gas plant, with appropriate storage. Possibilities include compressed-air energy storage using a large onsite natural salt dome, renewable hydrogen, large-scale flow batteries, and solid oxide fuel cells. Storage can help ensure that intermittent sources of power – such as wind – become grid-scale reliably.

Los Angeles has focused on shifting demand by commercial, industrial, and institutional customers from peak times to off-peak times. Those that sign up for the program develop plans to reduce their demand by a minimum of 100 kilowatts. When notifications are given for a demand-response event, participants enact their plans. LADWP ensures that demand-response events are no more than four hours long and that no more than twelve demand-response events occur per year. As incentives, participating businesses receive monthly payments in the hottest part of the year for every kilowatt reduction of energy use promised and also compensation for the energy they do not use during each event.

In 2018, 447 megawatts of electricity were conserved in this program by its forty-three participants. It has proven so successful that it will be automated by 2021. It is popular as well, with participating businesses being paid nearly US$500,000 in 2018. A demand-management program for residential properties (similar to that in Austin) will be added soon, and Los Angeles is also reviewing the potential for electric vehicles and smart meters to help with demand management.

Creative City Leadership

The strategies undertaken by LA and Austin are made possible because of public ownership of the electricity grid and the utility that generates power. The creativity with which they have both approached issues such as expanding solar suggests ideas that can be utilized by other cities, even if they do not own the utility. For example, cities can and do support solar and other programs through a variety of schemes, including their own purchasing of electricity, and use ways to generate heat or cooling that significantly reduce reliance on electricity or fossil fuels. Three interesting and effective initiatives are explored below.

City governments are using a variety of these types of methods to dramatically lower greenhouse gas emissions from the generation of electricity, even where they do not control the electricity grid or own the plants that generate electricity. In Vancouver, Canada, for example, heat is taken from sewer pipes through a heat exchanger and used to heat and cool buildings – thereby ensuring that those buildings do not need to use natural gas or electricity for that purpose. The underlying technology has been commercialized and is spreading rapidly in numerous cities globally.

Toronto has an interesting system by which it uses cold lake water instead of air conditioning to cool buildings. In the summer, cold water from Lake Ontario is piped from the lake to a network of public and private buildings in downtown Toronto, where, through a heat exchanger, the air is cooled. Known as Deep Lake Water Cooling (because water at the bottom of the lake stays the same temperature – just above freezing – year round), the system is owned by the utility EnWave.

Although now a private company, EnWave was originally a steam-heating cooperative owned by the City of Toronto, the University of Toronto, and the major downtown teaching hospitals. Subsequently the city bought out the shares of its partners and, as sole owner of EnWave, developed the Deep Lake Water Cooling concept. The system currently serves about seventy downtown office towers and public buildings – most of Toronto's downtown core – and is set for expansion. At inception, the system allowed office towers to end the utilization of electricity for air conditioning, which had a significant positive impact on greenhouse gas emissions. At that time, electricity for peak consumption – such as air conditioning on very hot days – was generated by a coal-fired power plant. Although in Toronto's case the coal plant is now closed, the principle remains that cities adjacent to a large body of water can have a technologically feasible, affordable, and clean source of cooling that does not rely on fossil fuels or electricity (except for small amounts of electricity needed to run pumps, etc.).

On the Climate Front Lines

Hong Kong, possibly learning from Toronto's success, has built a district cooling system in its Kak Tai district development. Unlike Toronto, though, Hong Kong uses seawater as the source of the cold water. It's an exciting development given that so many global megacities are adjacent to the ocean, as greenhouse gases from a district cooling system are minor and only reflect the electricity needed to run the pumps.

Similar principles exist with district energy – where multiple buildings are heated from a central power plant. EnWave, in Toronto, was originally incorporated as the Toronto District Heating Corporation to supply district energy to its partners – an efficient, cost-effective system. Today, we realize that such systems have a significant benefit for our climate as well.

An excellent example is in Copenhagen.

District Energy in Copenhagen: Efficient, Cheap Low-Carbon Energy

Copenhagen has one of the most ambitious climate mitigation plans of any city in the world: it plans to be carbon neutral by 2025 and entirely fossil fuel free by 2050. With about 60 per cent of its greenhouse gases coming from buildings, addressing the emissions associated with the electricity and heat used in buildings is essential. Copenhagen has a significant advantage here, as virtually all buildings in Copenhagen are connected to a district heating system. The system goes back almost to the turn of the last century but became critically important as a consequence of national policies enacted during the 1970s' oil crisis.

District energy is highly efficient and cost effective, and the policies that created it were farsighted. In the 1970s, Denmark ended its reliance on oil as a strategic choice – but moved to reliance on coal. Thus we have seen over the past twenty years a movement in Copenhagen to find other, cleaner sources of power to create electricity and power the district energy system.

In Copenhagen, power plants channel their waste heat into the district heating system. Electricity and heat production are therefore inextricably linked. Current fuel sources for these combined heat-and-power plants include coal, oil, natural gas, wind, biomass, geothermal, and waste. Wind energy is growing in Denmark, and Copenhagen aims to build one hundred new wind turbines by 2025. To build support for the turbines, the city has run awareness campaigns and offered tours of existing turbines, and it has also allowed citizens to invest in wind energy – a strategy that may well be key to public acceptance of the project, as Danes directly benefit financially from the clean energy generated by the turbines. (The Danes love co-ops. I was told a joke while in Copenhagen recently: "Two Danes get on the train to Copenhagen and by the time they arrive they have started three co-ops." I don't understand the joke, but it is illustrative of the concept.)

Recent strategies have focused on converting coal, oil, and natural gas plants to be capable of using biomass by the end of 2020. Biomass consists primarily of sustainably harvested wood pellets and straw, both of which are considered renewable and are carbon neutral. These power plants are essential complements to the wind and solar power plants as they can provide stable base loads and can change their power output rapidly to meet fluctuating demands.

One controversial area in Copenhagen is that waste incineration is also a major source of both energy and heat. The city is making an effort to address this issue by diverting waste, when possible, to better uses. Efforts to recycle and divert plastic from waste have therefore increased, as has the diversion of organic material from waste. These organics (together with sewage waste) are being used to generate biogas for use as a general fuel and in vehicles, and the city is actively working on its longer-term goal of eliminating the use of waste incineration entirely.

Copenhagen's district heat system is huge and complex. It includes over 1,500 kilometers of double pipes (incoming hot water/steam, outgoing cooled water/steam) and has separate operators for production, transmission, and distribution. Once in the building, heat exchangers are used to move the heat from the district system to the building's water-based heat system. The system is far more efficient than using a furnace or boiler in every home, which reduces emissions and also saves money: it is estimated that it would cost twice as much to heat the buildings in Copenhagen with conventional systems based on oil or natural gas, and the centralized system also allows for better pollution controls. Two small district cooling systems have also been added to the system. These use seawater and waste steam to help cool buildings.

These programs are working: by 2015, total greenhouse gas emissions were 38 per cent below 2005 levels, despite a 16 per cent growth in population. And with such a comprehensive long-term plan, Copenhagen is on track to achieve far more.

In the long term, beyond 2025, Copenhagen plans to move away from biomass, replacing those plants with geothermal energy and heat pumps. A large-scale heat pump pilot project that collects heat from seawater and wastewater was connected to the district heating system in 2019, and by 2025, the city plans to launch a large geothermal energy plant for clean energy.

District heating isn't an idea only for Denmark; it is a highly efficient and effective way to reduce the use of energy, even when powered by polluting sources – and, of course, is even more effective when a transition is made to clean energy sources as in Copenhagen.

It is an example of large-scale success at an urban level of innovation. Today, cities are testing geothermal, solar thermal, and other technologies in addition to the sewer-heat recovery mentioned above. All of these initiatives have significant potential to reduce reliance on fossil fuels and electricity to heat and cool buildings, or to generate clean electricity, and all are feasible – today.

The Final Word

City governments have demonstrated that a large-scale switch to renewable sources of generation is possible now, ending reliance on fossil fuels – at a minimum, drastically reducing the use of coal, oil, and natural gas to generate electricity. They have also demonstrated that through creative actions such as district heating and cooling, and emerging technologies such as heating from wastewater, the use of electricity from power plants can be dramatically reduced.

This leadership shows that arguments made by some that we have to keep relying on dirty power simply are not true. We know how to both generate clean electricity at scale and create systems that heat and cool our cities in ways that don't rely on fossil fuels at all. Through these methods our urban areas can see significant reductions in greenhouse gas emissions – according to McKinsey, up to 45 per cent reductions are possible using today's technologies and systems, right now. And in places where mayors cannot directly make the needed changes, they can use the power of city government to influence that change – just as Mayor de Lille in Cape Town and as the City of Toronto did, through innovative use of wind, solar, and deep-lake cooling.

Chapter 3

Existing Buildings

The Empire State Building in New York City is probably one of the most well-known buildings in the world. Built in the height of the Great Depression, it was the world's tallest building for nearly forty years. Its iconic architecture and famous history have kept it a symbol of the success of New York City and the United States of America. It is also an inspiring example of how it is economically feasible to dramatically reduce greenhouse gas emissions through smart city policies and a committed owner, who undertook a massive energy retrofit completed in 2011 and made other energy improvements. In doing so, the owner not only created jobs and dramatically lowered emissions but also paid back the investment in three years through savings from reduced costs and higher rents.

***

You can walk across the Brooklyn Bridge from Brooklyn to Manhattan. At sunset, the view is incredible. The world's most recognizable buildings, silhouetted against the sky. More or less straight ahead are the skyscrapers of the new World Trade Center, built to replace those tragically destroyed on September 11, 2001. Slightly to your right, the Empire State Building, the Chrysler Tower, the United Nations, and many others. At night, the dark sky is outlined against the lights of those same buildings, and you can see the lights of boats slowly moving below the bridge. And in the daytime, you are joined with a flood of people surging toward Manhattan.

When you get off the bridge, you're at city hall, a majestic marble building completed in 1812. City hall and the surrounding park are a small oasis of quiet and of green. Walk a few more blocks and you're in the midst of the narrow streets and tall buildings that are the southern tip of Manhattan. Buildings finished in the 1800s, grand though sometimes faded; buildings that seem as if they were finished last week – and probably were – and others built somewhere in between. You're surrounded by honking traffic, the ubiquitous yellow taxi cabs, buses, delivery vehicles, and you're standing on top of one of the world's great subway systems. You probably have a smile on your face because the energy of this busy city, the world's financial capital, is infectious. But mostly it's the buildings you notice, because you're surrounded by the results of an incredible building boom that has lasted nearly two hundred years. Manhattan is dense. Very dense indeed. Like walking through man-made valleys made of brick and glass.

Unlike the Empire State Building, many of these buildings do not meet the highest standards of energy efficiency. Studies show that if they did, New York's greenhouse gas emissions would plunge.

Why Buildings?

Manhattan is not alone. The buildings in that heavily built-up island matter very much in addressing climate change, although perhaps not in the public imagination. Many different responses to climate change have caught that imagination: using green

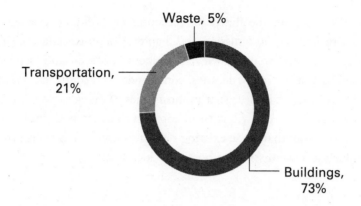

Figure 3.1: New York City's Greenhouse Gas Emissions, 2016
New York City's density translates into a higher proportion of emissions coming from buildings rather than transportation. Source: Based on data from City of New York, One City Built to Last: Transforming New York City Buildings for a Low-Carbon Future, *2016.*

energy, for example, often thought of as wind and solar; driving electric cars such as the Tesla; closing coal-fired electricity plants; planting trees; eating a meat-free diet; stopping the expansion of oil and gas projects; and more. But studies show that a significant part of our focus should be much more prosaic: the energy effi-ciency of buildings.

In large cities such as New York, the heating and cooling of build-ings can often be the major source of greenhouse gas emissions. We are not accustomed to thinking of our homes, our schools, our office buildings, and our commercial centers as creating pollution, but they do. We burn oil, gas, wood, and other fuels to heat our buildings, heat our water, cook our food. We use electricity, often generated by fossil fuels, to run just about everything. Though they don't have smoke-stacks, buildings are a major source of the emissions that cause cli-mate change. In cities, they can be the dominant source. Looking at the case of New York City, for example, a dense city where significant numbers of people take transit or walk to work, buildings rather than transportation are the leading source of greenhouse gas emissions by far: they alone accounted for 73 per cent as of 2016 (Figure 3.1).

We now have the ability to construct new buildings that operate with little or no emissions – Chapter 4 describes the exciting advances in that arena. However, our homes, offices, and factories generally last for many decades, sometimes even centuries. While estimates vary, it is clear that in most cities as many as 80 per cent of the buildings that will exist in 2050 have already been built. We need to ensure that these existing buildings use far less energy and produce as few emissions as possible – ideally zero.

Energy Consumption Can Be Dramatically Reduced in Buildings

How do we cut the carbon emissions from buildings to nearly zero? In theory, the market should be undertaking this on its own, as over the lifetime of a building, the reduction of its energy consumption (and therefore the cost of operation)' makes the building both more profitable and more valuable. But experience has shown that even though the economic case for dramatically improving the energy performance of buildings is strong, the work will not happen without leadership from government, most often from mayors and the city governments they run. Where they have legal authority, this leadership can be through regulations and mandates. Where they do not, leading cities have found highly effective ways to otherwise promote dramatic reductions in carbon emissions.

What must be done is conceptually clear. First, in the short term, the energy needed to operate buildings can be reduced through energy-efficiency retrofits, which is the focus of this chapter. Over time, as the electricity grid becomes clean, it will be possible to electrify all building operations, as Los Angeles is planning to do through its Green New Deal climate plan.

Most homes, offices, and institutional buildings today are heated and cooled with natural gas or oil. These fuels are the predominant source of emissions from buildings. Thus efficient energy use greatly impacts the overall consumption of fossil fuels and creation of greenhouse gases. Making these buildings more efficient involves significant technical work: improving the outside of the building (the "building envelope"), upgrading the electrical and mechanical systems – and rethinking how we behave.

Some context is needed here: buildings breathe. The climate generated inside escapes to the outside. Heat moves from warm areas to cool areas. It moves out of a warm building in winter and into a cool building in summer. The building envelope (a building's walls, windows, doors, foundation, and roof) is that building's main defense against heat loss or gain. Adding insulation, sealing air leaks, and replacing windows and doors are all important for making a building more energy efficient. These retrofits have an initial cost – but they are also the most effective way to reduce the total heating and cooling energy needs of a building and, over time, to save money from the reduced energy consumption.

A second critical area is a building's mechanical system. The biggest direct users of fossil fuels in a building are the systems that we use to heat the air and the water. These will use less energy when we improve the building envelope, but they can also be made more energy efficient themselves. Older boilers and furnaces are far less efficient at generating useful heat than newer models, and as they age, their performance may decrease through a lack of timely maintenance.

Addressing that performance decline is called retro-commissioning: the process of ensuring that all mechanical equipment and systems are operating optimally together. It's like cleaning and oiling your bicycle. With time, dirt and rust may accumulate in your gears, on your chain, on your bike cables. A tune-up once a year can ensure that your bike ride is smoother and takes less energy. A retro-commissioning of a building can resolve problems, improve its operation, and save energy.

Water use is often optimized alongside energy systems to save energy. When a building uses less hot water, it will also use less energy to heat that water. In large buildings, reducing water use can save energy by reducing the use of pumps to move water to the upper floors. Taps, showerheads, toilets, dishwashers, washing machines: all these devices can be upgraded to use less water and therefore less energy.

Even something as simple as changing a light bulb can save significant amounts of energy – when done at scale. An LED (light-emitting diode) light bulb can use 75 to 80 per cent less energy than an incandescent (traditional) bulb that produces the same amount of light. Those savings may be small for one light, but multiplied by the thousands of lights in a large office building, the savings become material. Replacing old lights with LED versions saves electricity and generates less waste heat: heat that must be removed with more air conditioning on hot days. And LED bulbs are far less costly to install and maintain. A large office building can save tens of thousands of dollars per year by modernizing its lighting systems, and with the falling cost of LED lights, the payback period is short.

Lights aren't the only thing to have become more energy efficient in recent years. Newer computers, printers, fridges, stoves, washing machines, and other appliances are all more energy efficient. New plumbing devices use less water and can save energy in heating and circulating water in a tall building. How many computers are there in an office building, and how many showers and fridges in a high-rise apartment building? Once again, the energy savings multiply when these changes are done at scale.

Not all energy-reduction measures involve adding or upgrading systems; some involve just rethinking how we use our buildings and how we approach heating or cooling. Monitoring how a building is used can lead to better programming of heating, cooling, and lighting systems. Painting a roof white can substantially reduce summer solar-heat gain, as can planting trees around a building. Waste heat from server rooms can be redirected to work areas in the winter. As we saw in Chapter 2, water from deep lakes and oceans can be used to keep our buildings cool. With the right incentives, building owners can be very creative in finding solutions. As examples throughout this chapter will show, cities have found ways to capitalize on that creativity.

The benefits of energy-efficiency retrofits go far beyond saving energy. Retrofitted buildings last longer. They are more comfortable because they're less drafty and have more even temperatures. They may even improve the indoor air quality. Energy-efficient buildings not only generate fewer climate-damaging emissions, they're also better work and living environments. Furthermore, lowering energy consumption in buildings has a clear economic case. The investments required are paid back through energy savings, making the building more profitable for the rest of its life. As we shall see, these savings can be impressive.

Barriers to Action

In fact, the economic case is so compelling that we must ask why these energy-reduction measures do not happen without government intervention. The story, from the perspective of a climate-change advocate, is familiar. And depressing. There are a variety of reasons – but all are rooted in short-term thinking caused by our economic system and not in the underlying costs and benefits. For example, some types of buildings are bought and sold frequently, causing many owners to focus on short-term costs rather than longer-term savings; owners may want to use their limited capital for other projects that have a more immediate payback; and the upfront costs and disruptions associated with retrofits can be a barrier. There is also the significant fact that owners and managers of buildings often do not pay the heating and cooling costs: tenants do. Therefore, if the owner bears the expense of improvements, it is the tenant who benefits from lower operating costs. (This is known as the split-incentive problem.)

But perhaps the biggest barriers to implementing energy-efficiency upgrades are inertia and lack of awareness of their benefits and co-benefits. Experience has proven that government intervention is imperative to overcome the structural barriers to action.

How, then, does a city ensure that building owners make buildings perform efficiently? Cities have started with persuasion – and have come up with some very innovative and successful strategies. Strategies that work.

Mayor Michael Bloomberg: Invoking the Power of the Market

New York City's inventory and analysis of its greenhouse gas emissions in 2005 revealed that buildings were responsible for close to 80 per cent of the city's total greenhouse gas emissions at that time. (To give some sense of magnitude, in 2005 New York City alone had emissions close to the total of those of all of Ireland or Switzerland.) What's more, the inventory showed that those emissions were rising, and the vast majority of the buildings responsible for that carbon pollution were expected to be still in use by the middle of the twenty-first century. Achieving the city's targets required a long-term, multistage plan to bring about major changes to the city's roughly one million buildings.

Benchmarking: Using Disclosure to Motivate Change

New York's former mayor Michael Bloomberg is fond of saying, "You cannot manage what you do not measure." This concept helped launch the city's benchmarking requirements for its largest buildings. Starting in 2010, all buildings of fifty thousand square feet or more were required to measure their energy and water use annually. This involved publicly disclosing both their energy and water use in addition to their building's Energy Star rating, a measure of building energy efficiency.

The advent of benchmarking meant that existing and prospective tenants could finally compare buildings for their energy performance and estimate the water and energy costs associated with renting a space. By making prospective tenants aware of utility costs, the New York benchmarking bylaw helped to address the split-incentive problem. For the first time, building owners started to become accountable to tenants for the efficiency of their buildings. Market forces meant that tenants started to choose more energy-efficient buildings – resulting in some significant and notable energy retrofits. As mentioned above, the owners of the Empire State

Building, for example, spent more than US$100 million on energy retrofits and have publicly stated that the efforts were extremely profitable as the modernized and energy-efficient building became popular, driving up rents.

New York chose the largest buildings first because those are the biggest users of energy and therefore provided the best opportunity for significant emissions reduction. The buildings required to disclose represented only 2 per cent of the roughly one million buildings in the city but used 45 per cent of the city's energy.

The benchmarking strategy was an important element in the city's Greener, Greater Buildings Plan but it was not the only measure taken. Starting in 2009, any new major renovations or building alterations were required to meet tougher energy codes. In addition, every year 10 per cent of all benchmarked buildings were required to undergo comprehensive energy audits and retro-commissioning. Finally, lighting and submetering upgrades were required of many benchmarked buildings. To support these actions, New York City established outreach and training programs, and created a benchmarking help center. Step by step, buildings were encouraged to take action to reduce their energy and water usage.

These measures were effective. By 2015, New York City buildings were emitting 18 per cent less greenhouse gases than they were just ten years earlier. By 2017, buildings owned and operated directly by the city itself had a 22 per cent improvement in their Energy Star ratings over 2010 levels and they were using 30 per cent less energy than they were in 2005.

The benchmarking plan demonstrated that it was effective in reducing energy use and greenhouse gas emissions from large buildings. In 2018, the program was expanded to include more buildings: the minimum size was lowered to twenty-five thousand square feet.

The success of the benchmarking plan in New York has also helped other cities. Chicago, Los Angeles, Houston, Phoenix, and Philadelphia, among others, have all included benchmarking as a strategy to encourage lower energy use in commercial buildings. In fact, an entire industry sector has been mobilized to help building owners, cities, and other organizations measure and track the energy performance of buildings. It is an effective first step to building a culture of energy efficiency – and the market skills to deliver results.

In New York City, the data creation and the years of tracking the energy use of buildings before and after retrofits has been invaluable for planners. Computer models generated from this data show the energy-efficiency gains that can be achieved with different measures in various building types. New and future policies are being developed from these models to target the buildings and the retrofit measures that will have the most impact for the least cost.

Energy models have shown that the most cost-effective measures of low to medium difficulty can generate a one-third reduction in emissions from the buildings sector. More comprehensive retrofits can achieve an estimated 40 to 60 per cent reduction in greenhouse gas emissions. It is also possible for these buildings to achieve net zero emissions, but they will need to meet all their remaining heating, cooling, and operational needs with electricity generated from carbon-free sources.

The benchmarking data has given owners, tenants, and city officials a greater understanding of the energy and water use of their buildings and the best strategies to become more efficient. It has also revealed that government leadership is still needed if the sector is to move as quickly as science requires to lower greenhouse gas emissions.

Beyond Benchmarking: The New York City Building Mandate

Under the leadership of current mayor Bill de Blasio, New York City released its updated climate plan, the Green New Deal, in 2019. Under the plan's rules, the city requires the worst performing of its benchmarked buildings to reduce annual emissions. Over time, benchmarking has been highly successful for the best buildings, where sophisticated tenants pay high rents and are in a position to choose between buildings. However, the approach has not had the same success in more modest buildings, for a variety of reasons: for example, owners may be anticipating profiting by short-term resale of the building and are not interested in investing for a future payback. The plan therefore takes a regulatory approach and mandates that by 2024, the highest-emitting buildings (the worst 20 per cent) must take measures to cut their energy use to bring their emissions below a mandated cap. By 2030, three-quarters of benchmarked buildings will be required to take action to meet their emissions caps.

Buildings can achieve their emissions caps through various means, the simplest and preferred being energy-efficiency upgrades. If those measures are impractical or insufficient to meet the targets, building owners have the option of fuel switching (to reduce the carbon intensity of their energy needs) and buying green-power credits. Up to 10 per cent of their annual emissions limit can come from the purchase of carbon offsets. Plans are also in development to introduce a carbon-trading system for buildings.

Buildings that don't reach their energy-efficiency targets by their deadlines will be fined – the level of sanction depending on the level of emissions. Large, inefficient buildings that do not comply could face millions of dollars in fines per year, a cost that is designed to be greater than the cost of compliance. The goal is a 40 per cent cut in emissions below 2005 levels by 2030 and net zero by 2050.

The challenges of paying the upfront costs of energy-efficiency retrofits were directly addressed by New York City in its climate plans under both Mayor Bloomberg and Mayor de Blasio. In 2011, New York City launched a nonprofit corporation to provide low-cost loans for energy and water efficiency retrofits in large commercial and residential buildings. In 2020, Property-Assessed Clean Energy (PACE) financing will be added as another option for commercial, industrial, nonprofit, and multiunit residential properties.

PACE loans are long-term, low-interest loans that cover energy-efficient equipment upgrades and installation of onsite renewable-energy systems. These loans are paid back through property taxes (from a building-owner's perspective, utilizing the energy savings created by the upgrades). PACE programs have been implemented in numerous communities and regions since the first program was introduced in Berkeley, California, in 2008. Communities across Canada, Europe, and Africa have advanced their own similar financing schemes – a good example of a program developed in one community being adapted and applied elsewhere to generate impressive results.

In total, required retrofits in New York City are expected to require the investment of US$4 billion. Much of those costs will be recovered by the building owner through utility savings in the coming years. In addition, the retrofit mandate is projected to create more than twenty-six thousand new jobs while improving buildings, increasing the comfort of the occupants, and reducing emissions.

To see how this might work, it is worth looking at the Empire State Building in detail. It is the most famous building in New York City. Opened by President Hoover in 1931, the office building has seen significant work during its long history, but none as important to its long-term sustainability as the energy-efficiency upgrades that began in 2009.

These were no simple fixes. All 6,514 windows were refurbished, insulation was added to the walls behind radiators, the chiller plant was upgraded, new controls were added to building-management systems, meters were replaced, submetering was introduced, and a web-based tenant energy-management system was introduced. The building utilized almost every technique that exists: better insulation, air sealing, mechanical equipment, and rethinking how energy is used. In 2013, these retrofits were saving US$2.8 million in operating costs per year, an energy savings of more than 40 per cent!

This will not be the end of the story. The Empire State Building was constructed at a time when energy efficiency, insulation, and airtightness were not the design considerations they are today, so to meet the new standards of the building mandate, the owners will likely need to consider the fuel switching, green-power credits, and offset options. But we know from the work done already that making significant efficiency gains even in an iconic building like this is not only technically feasible, but there is a business case for it too.

Other cities are grappling with the challenge with creative and effective programs – in both mandatory and non-mandatory ways.

> *"We gave people a very fair amount of time in the private sector to come forward and really agree to voluntary goals that will be sufficient. But time was up ... It was time to move to mandates."*
>
> **– Mayor Bill de Blasio (New York), 2019**

Urban Cap and Trade: Tokyo

Buildings are the biggest source of greenhouse gas emissions in Tokyo: 47 per cent of the city's carbon pollution was attributed to commercial and industrial buildings in 2015.

Like New York City, Tokyo has used mandatory reporting of greenhouse gas emissions from buildings as the basis for its program to meet climate-mitigation goals. Similarly, Tokyo has also focused on its largest buildings first. But rather than mandating the worst performers to meet energy-efficiency targets, Tokyo uses a cap-and-trade program to reach emission targets. This system promotes long-term thinking, rewards the best performers, and encourages innovation.

Mandatory reporting of building emissions began in 2002. Since that year, large buildings have been required to publicly report on their energy use and calculate carbon dioxide emissions every year. These buildings have also been required to prepare an emission-reduction plan. Classification as a large building in this program is based on total energy use and includes approximately 1,300 buildings. These facilities account for 20 per cent of the city's total emissions. In 2005, the posting of a building's energy and emissions rating was added to the list of requirements. But

implementing the submitted emission-reduction plan was voluntary, and by 2006, most building owners were taking only small
measures to reduce their carbon footprint. Tokyo decided that it was
necessary to develop a rules-based strategy that would drive much
greater carbon reductions.

Cap and Trade

Tokyo's cap-and-trade system for large commercial and industrial buildings was introduced in 2010. It was only the third
emission-trading scheme in the world and the first in Asia and –
unlike some examples that have been canceled with a change in
government – it is still in place. Using emissions from 2009 as a
baseline, targets were set with four-year compliance periods. The
first target was a 6 to 8 per cent reduction by 2014. By 2019, the target was 15 to 17 per cent, and it is anticipated that the 2020 to 2024
target will be a 25 to 27 per cent reduction below 2009 levels. Unlike
New York City's plan, these targets apply to every building.

Compliance with building-emissions targets is the responsibility
of the building owner, and the program encourages long-run thinking. Building owners must designate a general manager who helps to
chart a path toward lower energy use. There are no mandatory measures, so individual building owners can take their own approach. In
this way, energy-efficiency measures can be incorporated into existing
plans for equipment renewal, renovations, and regular maintenance.

For example, when replacing aging heating equipment, a building owner must now consider both the upfront cost and how that
equipment will help or hinder efforts to meet longer-term emissions
targets. Replacing the current heating system with a similar one
may lock in emissions for years to come, forcing a building owner
to also undertake more costly retrofits to meet future reduction
targets. A more expensive alternative heating system may therefore be the more cost-effective choice when all factors are considered. Emissions targets change the cost-benefit analysis and favor
economically efficient solutions.

The system has a solution for buildings that are so difficult to improve that they cannot meet the targets: trading carbon credits. A building owner unable to meet the emission-reduction targets must buy carbon credits to make up the difference, and that is where the trade in "cap and trade" occurs.

There are five sources of building-emission credits in Tokyo's cap-and-trade system. First, buildings that exceed their targets can save up their credits for future years or sell them to those less-efficient buildings that fall short. Second, small- and medium-sized buildings can sell carbon credits earned through major energy-efficiency upgrades. These smaller buildings have also been required to post yearly energy and emissions data but have not yet been subjected to emission-reduction targets. Third, buildings that generate renewable energy (from rooftop solar, for example) can also sell carbon offsets. Fourth, mechanisms are in place to allow large facilities outside Tokyo to sell carbon credits based on their energy-efficiency gains and reductions in greenhouse gas emissions. Finally, Tokyo's cap-and-trade system is designed to work with the cap-and-trade system operating in the neighboring prefecture of Saitama, and carbon credits can move between the two.

The best-performing buildings are rewarded under this cap-and-trade system. Not only can they make money selling their excess carbon credits, but they can also qualify for reduced emission targets. In addition, recognizing that buildings that had already invested heavily in energy-efficiency measures would be at a disadvantage when reduction targets are a percentage of total energy used, Tokyo created "top-level" and "nearly top-level" designations. These facilities must demonstrate aggressive historical emission cuts and adoption of more than two hundred energy-saving measures. In return, these top-level buildings are issued lower emission-reduction targets, and their achievements are celebrated: a very important motivator in an honor-based society.

In 2019, the tallest building in Tokyo, Toranomon Hills, was designated a top-level facility for its energy-efficiency achievements. The building houses a hotel, residences, offices, conference space, and retail space, and has a main arterial road running underneath it. In addition to the mandatory energy-saving measures, the building installed LED light fixtures, added fifty kilowatts of solar panels, and uses a high-efficiency heat-source system. A large-scale thermal-storage tank supports the heating system.

At the same time, Tokyo takes a serious view of those building owners who do not comply. Facilities that miss their targets are ordered to take measures to reduce emissions by up to 1.3 times the target shortfall by a given deadline. If that deadline is missed, the building owner is charged the cost of carbon credits for all outstanding emissions shortfalls, fined up to several thousands of dollars, and their building is publicly labeled in violation of emissions targets.

Tokyo supports its benchmarking and its cap-and-trade programs through yearly feedback reports to building owners. These reports include energy and emission data for facilities of a similar size and use, diagnostics of the building's energy use, and recommendations for future energy-efficiency measures based on identified best practices. Building engineers and consultants are also available to promote and support energy-efficiency upgrades. Indeed, effective engagement and communication with stakeholders in the program has been cited as a critical factor in the program's success.

Of course, a building's energy use is not just a matter of equipment and insulation. How the people in those buildings use the equipment matters too. Much of the space in those large commercial buildings is leased, and reducing energy use requires tenants' cooperation. Tenants are therefore required to cooperate with building managers in monitoring and reducing energy use.

For example, tenants are required to take simple measures to reduce their energy use: turning off lights when not in use, choosing energy-efficient office equipment, and promoting energy-conservation measures. Tenants must also share energy-use data and meet regularly with building managers to set energy-saving targets and plan how to achieve them. Tenants who occupy large areas in a building must submit their yearly energy and emissions data as well as their reduction plans to Tokyo city administrators. In this way, energy efficiency is a goal not just for the owners and managers but also for all those who use a building.

Tokyo's carbon-reporting program allows prospective tenants to compare buildings based not just on their obvious features but also on their energy performance and projected energy bills. Buildings can qualify for the low-emission-building label, which is a major selling point for rented spaces and can be an incentive for building owners to implement energy-efficiency measures that help them compete for tenants.

Tokyo's greenhouse gas reductions were challenged by the 2011 earthquake and tsunami that devastated the Fukushima nuclear power plant. Prior to those events, nuclear power was generating 30 per cent of Japan's electricity; afterwards, all nuclear power plants were shut down due to public concerns about their safety. Thermal power plants that burned fossil fuels were used in their stead: a shift that caused Japan's and Tokyo's emissions to rise. Yet the earthquake also spurred innovations and collective action that helped the buildings sector address its emissions. When the nuclear power plants were shut down, backup systems were unable to make up the capacity deficit. In the year that followed, Tokyo experienced an energy crisis: there were scheduled rolling power cuts and mandated reductions in peak energy use. Seeking ways to minimize disruption to their businesses from the energy crisis, many building owners explored energy-efficiency measures. The energy crisis showed how measures taken to reduce emissions also created better buildings that are more resilient to power disruptions, a significant co-benefit with a lasting impact.

By 2017, buildings subject to the cap-and-trade program had reduced emissions by 27 per cent of 2009 levels – a near doubling of required reductions, with 78 per cent of buildings exceeding their targets. Interest in energy efficiency has risen among senior business managers, and the program has stimulated demand for many new technologies. The most commonly implemented measures were lighting upgrades and installation of efficient equipment for heating, air conditioning, and pumping. The cap-and-trade system spurred interest in and business for retrofit technologies, building energy-management systems, and energy-service companies.

The next challenge for Tokyo will be small- and medium-sized buildings, which since 2010 have been required to report their yearly energy and emissions data, their voluntary emissions targets, and their plans to achieve them. However, they are not yet part of the formal cap-and-trade system and have not shown the reductions of the larger buildings in energy use and greenhouse gases.

On the Climate Front Lines

In Qingdao, China, the city government has hopes for a low-carbon future but has also recognized that older residential buildings have low energy efficiency. The city has adopted a low-carbon development plan with ambitious goals and targets, and to meet these targets it has launched an extensive plan to undertake energy retrofits on a huge number of older residential buildings. It is undertaking this through financial incentives that award significant support if an energy retrofit is completed with significant energy reductions – and the owners of the buildings will keep the cost savings from reduced energy use. The project is the result of work with other Chinese cities and is supported by technical expertise arranged by C40 Cities. Qingdao estimates that nearly three hundred thousand metric tons of greenhouse gas emissions have been prevented thus far, and there is potential to more than double this amount. As the electricity saved is primarily generated by coal, not only are the greenhouse gas savings significant, but also residents are enjoying more days with better air quality.

Effective Voluntary Partnerships: Toronto and Sydney

Located on the shore of Lake Ontario, Toronto experiences cold winters and hot, humid summers. It is not a surprise, therefore, that heating, cooling, and operating its many buildings account for so much of its energy use and greenhouse gas emissions (45 per cent in 2016). The use of natural gas for space and water heating is responsible for the vast majority of these emissions, since most of Toronto's electricity is generated from emission-free sources. Toronto has recognized the need to improve the energy efficiency of the buildings located in the city (and to electrify their heating). And that it must do so for buildings of all types.

As described in Chapter 1, Toronto's climate plan, "Change Is in the Air," was adopted in 2007 after consultations with thousands of residents and stakeholders, and was updated in 2017.

The updated plan, "Transform TO," has set goals to significantly lower energy consumption in existing buildings. It is hoped that energy-efficiency upgrades in existing buildings will reduce energy use by 40 per cent by 2050, and 30 per cent of the city's total floor space will be connected to low-carbon heating and cooling. To fulfill these plans, nearly every building within the city will need to be transformed into a high-performing, energy-efficient space – but unlike New York City, Toronto does not have the legal power to compel building owners to take these steps. It has to rely on voluntary measures and on its own leadership.

The City of Toronto is demonstrating that leadership by maximizing energy efficiency in its municipal buildings. The city's target date for near zero energy consumption in its new municipal buildings is 2026, and it plans to reduce energy consumption in existing city-owned buildings by 40 per cent by 2040 (ten years ahead of the goal for other buildings in the city). The city already has implemented energy-conservation and demand-management practices in its more than six hundred buildings through the automation of building systems. All major buildings have undergone energy-efficiency retrofits, financed by the savings in energy costs. And city-owned facilities are installing solar panels with a goal of reaching twenty-four megawatts by the end of this year. This city leadership makes the implementation of voluntary programs in the private sector far easier.

Better Buildings Partnership: Toronto

Toronto's current climate plan builds on a program developed two decades earlier. In 1996, the Better Buildings Partnership (BBP) was launched to promote energy-efficiency retrofits in large private residential, commercial, industrial, and institutional buildings, and has been highly successful in reducing energy consumption, particularly of natural gas. As the name suggests, the BBP is a partnership – between energy-management firms, utilities, and the City of Toronto. The work of the partnership has evolved as best practices have evolved elsewhere; today, for example, the BBP makes use of an energy and water reporting and benchmarking program, which is an idea borrowed from New York City. To date, through this voluntary program, more than 2,600 buildings have undertaken energy retrofits and reduced greenhouse gases by more than 810,000 metric tons annually.

Toronto is also addressing residential properties such as single-family homes. Investing in residential energy- and water-efficiency retrofits or renewable-energy projects with payback periods longer than people expect to live in their homes might not make economic sense for a particular occupant, even though it does overall for the property. To address this challenge, Toronto has created the Home Energy Loan Program. These long-term, low-interest loans are tied to the property, not the property owner. This means that when a home is sold, the new beneficiary of the efficiency upgrades is also responsible for making the remaining payments for those retrofits. As part of the application process, all homes must undergo a home-energy assessment, and the owner is provided with recommendations for cost-effective improvements and information about available rebates and incentives. Another home-energy assessment is conducted after the retrofits to verify and quantify the efficiency gains. (These loans are another form of PACE financing.)

Toronto is also addressing the energy efficiency of high-rise residential buildings, particularly those built between 1960 and 1980, when building codes had significantly lower standards of energy efficiency. It takes serious planning and upfront investment to retrofit a high-rise apartment building. Two programs have been developed to support these buildings in undertaking retrofits: High-Rise Retrofit Improvement Support (Hi-RIS) and Energy Savings Performance Agreements (ESPAs).

Hi-RIS is another PACE-type program specifically designed for residential apartments of three or more stories. Energy-efficiency, water-efficiency, and renewable-energy projects can be financed at low cost for up to twenty years through this program. Utility savings offset the retrofit costs, and energy and greenhouse gas emissions reductions are verified through comprehensive energy audits. As in similar programs, the loans are tied to the property, not the property owners.

An ESPA is a service-performance agreement in which a third party pays for the energy-efficiency retrofit and recoups its costs plus a small return through the resultant energy cost savings over the term of the agreement. Once the investment is repaid, all energy cost savings are enjoyed by the building owner. In Toronto, ESPAs can be arranged for large residential, commercial, and institutional buildings through a private corporation that partners with the Toronto Atmospheric Fund (TAF). TAF is a nonprofit created with an endowment from the City of Toronto to support and finance climate-action and clean-air initiatives in the city. ESPAs are marketed to building owners as budget neutral, as shown by the chart in Figure 3.2.

The Robert Cooke Co-op is an excellent example of the potential of ESPA financing. This affordable housing complex includes 28 townhomes and a 123-unit tower built in 1992. Being a co-op with subsidized units, there was little money available to invest in efficiency retrofits. The ESPA paid for high-efficiency space and water heaters, a better ventilation system, weather stripping, upgrades to lighting, new appliances, and water-efficiency upgrades. The retrofits were completed in 2013 and achieved a 30 per cent reduction in annual greenhouse gas emissions. The simple payback period for the retrofits was a mere five years, and the annual energy and cost savings exceeded expectations. What's more, the residents reported greater comfort in their homes after the retrofit, and the measures taken were expected to extend the lifespan of the buildings by twenty years.

Nearly all buildings in Toronto can apply for an energy-retrofit loan. These loans were first available only to city divisions, agencies, and community-based entities. By 2019, having proven its value in promoting retrofits, and to integrate the program goals with those of

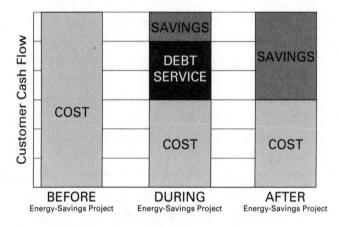

Figure 3.2: Energy Savings Performance Contracting
This figure shows how an Energy Savings Performance Agreement (ESPA)
works. Source: Based on AMERESCO, Performance Contracting: A
Budget-Neutral Solution, *www.ameresco.com.*

Transform TO, the loan program was expanded to include buildings of
nearly all types. The loans provided by the program can cover up to the
full upfront cost of an energy-efficiency retrofit or renewable-energy
project. During the application process, city staff also help building
owners access any incentives and rebates available from utilities and
other governments. The loans can extend for up to twenty years and
they have fixed, low-interest terms: interest rates are set at the city's
cost of borrowing. For most of the funded retrofits, the energy savings
over the loan period will be greater than the total cost of the loan.

By 2016, greenhouse gas emissions from the city were 33 per cent
below 1990 levels: 3 per cent better than and four years ahead of the
2020 target. Emission reductions in buildings that have undergone
retrofits have been significant, even though the new programs are
still at an early stage. These projects have demonstrated that major
cuts to energy costs and greenhouse gas emissions are possible from
all types of buildings.

All the retrofit financing programs described above have win-
win-win outcomes. Building owners get energy-efficiency upgrades
to their buildings that improve their performance, increase their
value, extend their life, and save the owners money over the long

term. Tenants and building occupants get more comfortable living and working spaces plus lower utility costs. The City of Toronto wins as emissions from buildings come down with programs that do not draw from the municipal budget: the loan and associated administration costs are generally covered in full by the loan repayments. What's more, retrofit programs create jobs – often good union jobs with decent wages and benefits – and economic opportunity.

> *"I think it is [a] dual focus: employing [the] energy consultants from low-income families, and through them we can make many humble homes energy-efficient. So it's like catching two birds with one stone."*
>
> **– Mayor Park Won-soon (Seoul), 2016**

All these programs are made possible because of strong partnerships between the city, building owners, and other stakeholders. These partnerships are essential for developing effective programs that meet the needs of all groups in a way that considers the unique challenges and opportunities of each city. Other cities have shown that the concept is easy to follow and can succeed.

Better Buildings Partnership: Sydney

Sydney launched its own Better Buildings Partnership in 2011. It is an important part of Sydney's plan to achieve net zero emissions by 2050. In a city where more than 80 per cent of greenhouse gas emissions come from the electricity used in buildings, improving the energy efficiency of buildings is essential to reducing emissions (see Figure 3.3).

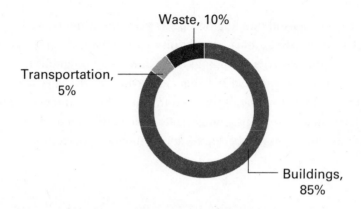

Waste, 10%

Transportation,
5%

Buildings,
85%

Figure 3.3: Sydney's Emissions Inventory
Buildings are by far the most significant source of greenhouse gas emissions in Sydney, Australia. Source: Based on data from Global Covenant of Mayors, Sydney, Australia, www.globalcovenantofmayors.org/cities/sydney/.

Sydney's BBP is a partnership between the city and a group of major commercial property owners and managers who together own or manage more than half the office floor space in the city center. They have developed collaborative approaches to improving the performance of their buildings, with an emphasis on energy, water, and waste. Many of their programs focus on information sharing, education, and toolkits.

For example, the BBP publishes information about "Green Leases." Using a scorecard, an owner's or a manager's willingness to work with tenants and take concrete steps toward sustainability is evaluated, based on identified best practices. Lease clauses that support these green practices are also published by the BBP. In this way, tenants and owners can work together to create a work environment that saves energy, reduces absenteeism, encourages greater employee retention, increases productivity, and saves significant costs.

A simple and cost-effective sustainability measure promoted by this program is changing the building temperature controls so that office temperatures are a few degrees warmer in summer than in winter, and expanding the temperature range over which the heating or cooling systems turn on or off. A building might set the temperature in winter to 21°C (70°F) with the heating coming on at 20°C

(68°F), and shutting off at 22°C (72°F). In summer, the temperature may be set to swing between 24°C (75°F) and 26°C (79°F). This simple measure can save up to 30 per cent on heating and cooling costs.

Sydney's Smart Green Apartments program addresses residential high-rises. Energy and waste assessments are provided at no charge by the city and form the factual basis for the creation of action plans, training, and implementation support to make apartment buildings more water and energy efficient.

Sydney also supports building recommissioning, which it calls building tune-ups. These help improve the performance of the mechanical and electrical systems in a building and can save an owner thousands of dollars per year with a low-cost investment. Along the way, the city helps to connect building owners with incentive programs and will subsidize the installation of automated systems for monitoring and controlling usage.

One example of what has been done in Sydney is at the Regis Towers Complex, which consists of three residential high-rise towers built in 1998. Each tower has its own sports facility and pool, and together they comprise more than 650 apartments. By installing more energy-efficient fans and motors, and by adjusting the settings of timers and sensors, building owners were able to reduce their energy bills by 37 per cent. Adding smart water-monitoring technology saved more than AUD$35,000 per year by allowing managers to address leaks and other problems early – an important example of simple, relatively inexpensive measures having significant results.

Building retrofits in Sydney are supported through a variety of financing programs. Funding for energy-efficiency projects that reduce greenhouse gas emissions is available from federal and state programs. There are grants available from the city for innovation, operations, and energy assessments.

The City of Sydney has a PACE-type financing program with some notable differences from the one operated by Toronto. The program is called Environmental Upgrade Finance (EUF). Like Toronto's Hi-RIS program, it offers long-term, low-interest loans for up to the full cost of energy-efficiency upgrades and solar projects. As in Toronto, the loans are tied to the property, and repayments are collected through city billing. Unlike the Toronto program, a third-party lender provides the capital, and the program addresses the split-incentives problem: a major barrier to retrofits in commercial buildings.

As noted above, building owners have little incentive to pay for retrofits when it is their tenants who realize the economic savings. Provisions were therefore made in Sydney's EUF to make it possible for tenants to be partially responsible for loan repayments. Tenant contributions cannot exceed their energy-bill savings, but they still benefit from the improved indoor environmental conditions that the retrofits provide. Tenants are therefore also incentivized to support the energy-efficiency upgrades that enhance their work environment at no additional net cost.

St James' Hall in Sydney is an interesting case study. Built in 1963 on the site of a former concert hall of the same name, St James' Hall is a thirteen-story office and retail building owned by the Anglican Church. In 2014, the building underwent major retrofits, including replacing chillers, installing energy-efficient fans and motors for the ventilation system, adding a building operation management system, and upgrading lighting. Approximately 40 per cent of the total project financing costs is being paid through tenant contributions, without increasing the total cost to lease the space. Churchwarden James Balfour has commented, "The project provides benefits for our tenants as well as for us and for the environment. It's a win-win-win."

The Better Buildings Partnership has generated some impressive results to date. While Sydney's overall emissions had seen a 17 per cent drop by 2015, emissions from the building spaces that participated in the BBP realized a 45 per cent drop over that same period.

The Final Word

One of the most effective ways to lower greenhouse gas emissions in any urban area is to address greenhouse gas emissions from existing buildings. The amount depends on the city type – a large, built-up city such as New York or Tokyo will have proportionately better results than a spread-out city – but in all cities the energy efficiency of buildings matters greatly. It has been proven that by starting with the buildings with the highest emissions and using a regulatory approach where that power exists, and a voluntary one where it doesn't, a city can dramatically lower emissions from the heating and cooling of buildings. The McKinsey *Focused Acceleration* report tells us that energy retrofits can reduce greenhouse gas emissions in an urban area by 20 to 55 per cent – an incredible contribution, and one that often creates significant employment at the same time. The main challenge in ensuring that these actions happen rapidly and at scale is not financial and technical; it is that in many places city governments do not have the legal authority to require change and therefore depend on the use of voluntary programs such as those in Toronto and Sydney – which, while extremely effective, require a high rate of participation to reach the same levels of overall emissions reduction as mandatory rules such as those in New York's buildings mandate or Tokyo's cap and trade.

Chapter 4

New Buildings

Vancouver, British Columbia, is wedged on the west coast of Canada between the ocean and the mountains. It is sometimes thought by Canadians to be a bit like California – a place that moves to its own rhythms – occasionally called "the left coast" by some. As such, it often has been a source of innovation, as it is in forging techniques to build dramatically better buildings. In 2011, the University of British Columbia opened the Centre for Interactive Research on Sustainability, a net-positive building – actually helping draw down carbon emissions. Designed as a living laboratory, the building is also an educational project for students in engineering and architecture. It has anticipated an ongoing necessity for improvement and has provided an excellent way to assist in widely disseminating best practices about new building construction to the industry in British Columbia.

***

Downtown Vancouver is built on a peninsula. It's a beautiful piece of land, and long ago a farsighted decision was taken to protect the western-most end of that peninsula as a park – Stanley Park. It is surrounded by nearly ten kilometers (about six miles) of seawall, and it is possible to run, walk, or bike around the seawall. In doing so, the views are incredible – of snow-capped mountains behind North Vancouver; of the busy harbor; of the magnificent Lions Gate Bridge, which opened the north shore of Vancouver (the "British Properties") to development; of Siwash Rock mysteriously erect a few yards into the ocean; of ships moored waiting for cargo; of the beaches of English Bay; and then of downtown. When I run the seawall, I usually run clockwise, starting in English Bay and moving west and north. Running in that direction, when you come around the last corner of the park, the glory of downtown Vancouver opens up in front of you – the convention center with its sails and green roof and an array of new buildings, as far as you can see.

At least since the world's fair took place in Vancouver in 1986, the city has had a building boom downtown and in the adjacent neighborhood of False Creek. The number and scale of the buildings is significant – and illuminates a fundamental point about work to address climate change in cities. In cities such as Vancouver (and those in China), where there is significant construction and a modern building boom, how do we ensure that our newly constructed buildings are built in a way that secures a low-carbon future? The answer lies in the actions of city governments.

Planning Approvals and Building Codes

Central to the role of almost every city government is the task of guiding development – planning where new buildings should be; what uses are appropriate in different neighborhoods; and the size, height, and density of a proposed building. In different countries there are different rules, but such rule making is typically undertaken through planning approvals and a citywide development (or "Official") plan. It might say, for example, that tall skyscrapers

We can see the beauty of a modern building from many angles. But what matters from a climate-change perspective is often harder to see. Is the building insulated properly? Can it generate its own energy? Does it use its design to minimize the need for heating and cooling? Does the beautiful glass exterior hide an inefficient building that better design would have made energy efficient? Source: David East/Unsplash.

in a downtown core are welcome, but that abattoirs in a residential neighborhood are not; or that owners of single-family homes may convert their houses into duplexes, but that the building must still be about the same size as other houses in the neighborhood.

In many places, cities also control the building code – the rules that govern construction of new buildings. The twin tools of planning approval and approval over the methods of construction are powerful, as a city can then influence both the density of a city and how easy it is, for example, to travel between home and work or school, as well as the actual quality of construction. These powers have important environmental impacts – impacts that become critical in the growing cities of China (and soon Africa and India), where new buildings can make or break a long-term climate-action plan. They can be built to conventional standards that use carbon-intensive materials and lock the building in to high operational-energy needs that will be hard to address later. Alternatively, they can be thoughtfully designed to use carbon-storing materials and generate zero emissions during their operation.

It is possible today to mandate that new buildings be designed to fit the latter criteria: to be energy efficient, to use less carbon-intensive materials, to use technologies that generate little or no emissions, and to adopt new passive-energy strategies (passive energy is also a very old-fashioned idea). When these measures are done well, to the highest of modern standards, a new building can be part of the climate solution rather than part of the problem: buildings can be a net carbon sink. Before discussing the leading examples of how cities are making this happen, it is useful to understand some facts about constructing new energy-efficient buildings.

Green Operating Building Standards

Constructing a new building to use very little energy to operate is much easier than retrofitting an existing building to the same standards. Indeed, it is now possible to design new buildings to produce as much renewable energy as they use over the course of a year: these are usually called net-zero-energy buildings. Buildings can also be constructed to generate no net emissions in operation: these are called net-zero-emission buildings, or zero-carbon buildings. Since buildings last for decades, it is critical that the buildings we put up now not lock us in to continued emissions that may be difficult to reduce or offset later. There are several green building standards that exist with different criteria – for example, the work done by Green Building Councils internationally. This chapter will explore what is currently possible and being undertaken in cities today.

Zero-carbon buildings operate using systems that generate no net emissions from the building operations. These buildings are often heated with electric heat pumps or with biogas-based district heating systems. The electricity supplied to these buildings must come from renewable-energy sources, either on- or off-site. As we saw in Chapter 2, many utilities now offer contracts for electricity generated from renewable sources.

Net-Zero-Carbon Buildings

By definition, net-zero-carbon buildings must be designed to use as little energy as possible in their operations. That means designing buildings with effective insulation, an airtight building envelope, and high-performance windows. It also means using high-efficiency equipment and giving careful attention to how the occupants will use energy.

Fortunately, energy-efficient options exist for many building components. The field of building science has exploded in recent years, as demand grows for energy-efficient, healthy buildings. Zero-carbon buildings can now be designed and built with greater ease and less cost.

Does building to high energy efficiency cost more? Yes. Typically, the cost of construction will be higher. Nonetheless, the cost of operation will certainly be lower. There are multiple reasons builders generally have not built to the highest technically possible building standards – the single biggest is that the costs of construction are paid by the constructor of the building, but the operating savings accrue to the future owners or to the tenants of the buildings. The problem of such split incentives means that regulatory intervention is critical to correct the market failure. However, as architects, construction workers, and suppliers gain knowledge and experience the added cost of building to high energy-efficiency standards is decreasing. But even if it were not, today any extra construction costs are paid back relatively quickly through operating savings – and those savings continue for the rest of the building's life.

The split-incentive problem does not apply to institutions or businesses that build anticipating that they will own the building for its lifespan. Thus we often see governments further ahead in energy efficiency in new construction than the private sector, as the cost incentives – lower lifetime cost, including the cost of operations – are aligned with energy efficiency. A nice example is in Cambridge, Massachusetts, which in addition to doing interesting work with a consortium of local businesses and institutions on a collective approach to net-zero buildings, recently opened the King Open and Cambridge Street Upper Schools Campus.

The campus includes two schools, offices, a public library, a community center, and other amenities. Using advanced energy efficiency, solar energy, geothermal heating, and a rainwater-reclamation system, the project is close to net zero – and will become net zero as the local energy grid becomes cleaner.

On the Climate Front Lines

Significant strides are being made in several cities to rapidly move to zero-emission buildings – in fact London, England, under the leadership of Mayor Sadiq Khan, has required zero-carbon homes since 2016 and now requires all new development to be zero carbon. Those builders whose buildings are unable to reach the targets are required to pay into an offset fund overseen by the city. As most cities have development responsibility, such initiatives have potential to scale up globally – as does a new policy adopted by Honolulu to encourage the use of low-carbon concrete in all new projects in the city. It is estimated that up to 8 per cent of global emissions of CO_2 come from concrete, so Mayor Kirk Caldwell has undertaken to lead the city to use CO_2 mineralized concrete, in which CO_2 that would otherwise escape to the atmosphere – for example, from a power plant – is used to harden the concrete. The process creates both a better concrete and a way to sequester carbon. In Honolulu, the city's purchasing impact is such that the market for concrete is likely to change to entirely mineralized carbon because the small number of suppliers will need to adapt their plants and processes to bid for city work. This action can easily be replicated by cities (and concrete suppliers) globally.

New Technologies

Technologies are also evolving. Electric heat pumps capable of reaching average efficiencies of 300 per cent and more are now available. It is difficult for a non-engineer like me to understand how 300 per cent efficiency is possible, but it's due to the nature of heat pumps. Heat pumps move heat rather than generating it and are therefore capable of greater than 100 per cent efficiency. Even in cold Canadian winters, heat pumps can extract heat energy from the outside and use it to keep a building warm. And in summer, they move heat out of the building, replacing the need for a separate air conditioner.

There are improved designs to many aspects of a building – windows, insulation, lighting, control systems – but one relatively new technology that has captured attention is using heat pumps to extract energy from wastewater and sewage. The technology is relatively simple and has been piloted in a number of cities, including Vancouver, and Galashiels and Glasgow, Scotland. Its virtue is that it turns waste into a useable product – heat – simply and inexpensively, and moreover uses heat sources (wastewater and sewage waste) that have not been traditionally thought of as a resource, which exist in all buildings, and are renewable.

Modern Passive Design

New technology is not the only solution. There are many building techniques that use cheap and easy passive-design principles to reduce the need for energy-based systems. The South African cities of Cape Town, Durban, Johannesburg, and Tshwane have all committed to using passive-design standards to ensure that all new buildings are zero carbon by 2030.

Buildings form a significant share of emissions for these South African cities, and energy use for air conditioning in their hot climate is a major consideration, particularly as the South African energy grid depends to a significant proportion on coal. South Africa also struggles with high unemployment and very high poverty rates, as well as with one of the world's worst levels of income inequality. Building to tough green standards is often perceived as expensive and only for those who can afford it. Consequently, the four South African cities are investing heavily in stakeholder engagement and education and awareness campaigns, in addition to finding affordable solutions. Their energy-efficient building strategies place a huge emphasis on passive-design principles (some of which are described below). These techniques are generally cheap and easy and can be used anywhere.

Color matters to passive design. In the same way that a sidewalk can get very hot on sweltering summer days, dark surfaces on buildings will absorb more heat than light-colored ones. This is true of all surfaces, and significant work has been done to create cool roofs – by designing roofs to reflect the sun's rays. Many different cool-roof materials are now available, from asphalt shingles to steel roofs to spray-foam flat roofs to white-painted roofs, and more. Cool roofs don't even need to be white: highly reflective darker cool-roof materials are available. And while cool roofs reduce the need for air conditioning in the summer months, they do not have a negative effect on the need for heat in the winter. Green roofs, designed to use rainwater and sunlight to feed plants, are also a passive way of keeping a building cool in summer while absorbing heat through transpiration and storing carbon in plants, and in the right locations can function as an above-ground private or public park.

It is also possible to use the siting and orientation of a building to control heat accumulation from the sun and create more comfortable buildings, an approach used in ancient times as well as more recently. The idea is enjoying renewed interest and adoption in South Africa and elsewhere. "Solar gain" comes from direct exposure to the sun's rays. The sun moves from east to west and passes high in the sky in the summer months. In winter, the sun arcs closer to the southern horizon in the northern hemisphere and closer to the northern horizon in the southern hemisphere. Careful orientation of a building and siting of the windows can substantially reduce passive heat gain and the need for air conditioning in the summer. That same orientation can maximize passive heat gain in the winter. This measure costs next to nothing to implement but generally fell out of favor in the post-war building boom of the 1950s and 60s at a time of cheap energy. Furthermore, the use of overhangs, louvers, blinds, plants, and other window-shading features can also help to control solar-heat gain. Finally, careful window placement can be used to reduce the need for electric lighting with its associated waste heat. Creating comfort for building occupants can mean designing better buildings, and in the process using far less energy.

I recently visited an interesting building in Waterloo, Ontario, that is well on its way to being a certified zero-carbon building. It is a three-story office building with solar panels over the parking lot, a ground-source heat pump, a grey-water system, and a very nice green wall. But the feature that impressed me the most is one that's hard to see: the solar wall. It looks like a normal dark metal siding on the south side of the building. There are small holes drilled into the siding and behind it is an air-filled cavity. Air enters through the holes and is warmed when the sun hits the dark metal. That warm air rises and is drawn into the heating system in winter. The heating system therefore uses far less energy to heat the building as the incoming fresh air is already pre-heated by the sun. On a sunny day last winter, when the outside temperature was −13°C (9°F), air entering the building through the solar wall hit 16°C (61°F). Twenty-nine degrees Celsius (52°F) of free heat on a cold winter day!

Finally, buildings can benefit from passive ventilation. Having windows that open and spaces that connect from one side of a building to another allow for cross-breezes that can do much to improve the comfort and air quality of a building. Warm air rises, and when openings are placed at the top and bottom of a building, the warm air escaping at the top can draw in cooler air at the bottom, a process often called the stack effect. This technique was used in the architecture of Ancient Iran to keep buildings cool.

These various possibilities illustrate that there are many considerations when designing new buildings for lower carbon emissions. Fascinating examples of city leadership on building standards demonstrate inspired action is possible – now.

Leadership that Works: Vancouver

Vancouver declared a climate emergency in April 2019 and directed city public servants to draft a strategy to address the emergency. The *Climate Emergency Response* report that followed outlined six "big moves" and fifty-three accelerated actions. Vancouver's previous goal of reducing emissions by 80 per cent over 2007 levels by 2050, for example, was replaced with a greater (and scientifically required) ambition to become carbon-neutral by 2050. In the buildings sector, which in 2017 represented 59 per cent of the city's total emissions, Vancouver has made significant progress, and its approach to new buildings is particularly noteworthy.

Vancouver is the most expensive place to buy a home in Canada. And with a growing population, demand for real estate is likely to remain high for quite some time. It is estimated that 40 per cent of the buildings that will exist in Vancouver in 2050 will be built after 2020, with the majority of this new development being residential (see Figure 4.1). To address the climate consequences of this building boom, Vancouver has pledged to have all new buildings be constructed to net-zero-carbon standards by 2030. In addition, Vancouver has committed to addressing embodied carbon (the carbon in building materials, such as concrete) as

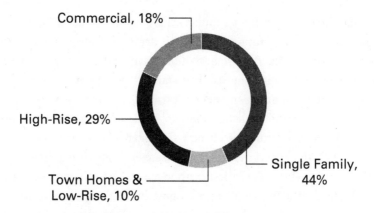

Commercial, 18%

High-Rise, 29%

Town Homes &
Low-Rise, 10%

Single Family,
44%

Figure 4.1: Vancouver's Built Area by Building Type, 2020
Vancouver has a variety of building types – note the significant number of high-rise buildings (nearly 30 per cent). Source: Based on data from City of Vancouver, Zero Emissions Building Plan, *July 2016.*

well: the city-council-approved goal is to reduce embodied carbon from new buildings and construction projects by 40 per cent below 2018 levels by 2030.

Net-Zero-Carbon Building Strategy: Vancouver

In Vancouver, by 2015, greenhouse gas emissions from the operation of new single-family homes had been cut to half of 2007 levels through prescribed energy-efficiency measures. The targets for cuts to emissions from new buildings are set to increase incrementally until all new buildings are net zero carbon in their operations by 2030. Building bylaws support these reductions with performance targets for every major building type. These metrics measure annual greenhouse gas emissions, energy used for heating, and total energy used – all normalized to the size of the building.

The building standard that Vancouver favors (but does not mandate) for the residential sector is the Passive House standard. Structures built to this internationally recognized standard are so well insulated and airtight that their heating and cooling needs are minimal. Even in colder climates, most homes built to this standard could be heated by a heat output equivalent to that of a hair dryer. Small heat pumps connected to the ventilation system that brings in fresh air can easily meet all heating and cooling needs. This standard is supported by professional training programs, modeling software, and a third-party verification process. While Vancouver has not made achieving passive-house certification mandatory for all new detached houses, achieving very high standards of energy efficiency and zero emissions is required – and this standard will be the easiest method of achieving these targets.

Instead of using heat pumps, some homes may be able to use neighborhood renewable-energy systems. These district heat and cooling systems offer economies of scale for converting whole neighborhoods to 100 per cent renewable energy. They can use low-cost energy sources, such as waste heat from sewers and commercial or industrial centers or wood waste that is not contaminated with other materials like nails – known as "clean wood waste." As Vancouver is a major exporter of lumber, the area is a great source of clean wood waste. These district energy systems are being expanded, and the proportion of energy they use from renewable sources is increasing.

Even with electrified heat systems, there are still emissions to consider. The electricity supplied to Vancouver is more than 97 per cent renewable, with most of the energy coming from hydroelectric dams. When electric heat and hot-water systems are used, buildings will be required to offset the small carbon footprint from electricity with onsite renewable energy systems or, if this is not feasible, by purchasing energy from other Vancouver-based renewable sources.

The shift to carbon-neutral buildings is supported by the center for excellence for zero emissions buildings, which shares information and best practices. It also helps suppliers of relevant building components (such as windows) and people in the building industry itself develop the skills necessary to expand capacity and to meet the zero-emission goal. Since the step-wise performance targets for buildings are known well in advance, suppliers, manufacturers, and the building industry are able to plan and build the capacity needed to meet future targets. The center also engages with the public to strengthen market demand for energy-efficient buildings.

Addressing Embodied Carbon

One of the many things that stands out in Vancouver's plans is its attention to embodied carbon emissions. While efficiencies reduce the energy a building needs for its operations, concern remains about emissions associated with construction materials, which are part of a building's carbon footprint. Currently more than half the lifetime emissions from an energy-efficient building may be emitted even before the doors open for the first time. Reducing these emissions is crucial to global efforts to limit warming from greenhouse gases. Since 2017, builders have been required to report embodied emissions in their projects. As reporting shifts to mandated reductions, bylaws and incentives are being developed to support the new design and building practices required.

Vancouver has been working with the construction industry, engineers, and other experts to devise realistic approaches to reducing embodied carbon, including the use of mass timber construction, lower-carbon concrete, and techniques to reduce the amount of concrete, steel, and aluminum needed. This continued experimentation and innovation is critical to show that it is possible – technically and economically – to reduce the embodied carbon in new buildings. Vancouver is leading the way.

A proposed thirty-three-story high-rise residential building was used as a model by City of Vancouver public servants for calculating embodied-carbon emissions. It allowed for a closer look at how embodied-carbon considerations might affect a building's design. In the model, the calculated embodied carbon for building using standard materials was set as the baseline. The calculated effects of different design changes and material switches on embodied carbon were compared to this baseline. The goal was to achieve Vancouver's climate target of a 40 per cent reduction in embodied carbon below 2018 levels by 2030.

Achieving a 40 per cent reduction in this case study required many measures, but the goal was attainable with current building techniques – no invention of new technologies or components was required. These measures included the use of low-carbon concrete, the replacement of carbon-intensive aluminum with steel, and either the use of precast hollow-core floor slabs or a 50 per cent reduction in underground parking. Combining all measures resulted in a modeled 47 per cent reduction in embodied-carbon emissions. Although a reduction in parking might require a change in municipal bylaws that, as in most cities, mandate a certain amount of parking for buildings, that too could work in Vancouver's favor as it strives to create a more walkable city, with low emissions from transportation. That would be a significant positive synergy – but even if the building does not assist in that goal, the overall effect of the new rules is a building that, by using simple changes to design, generates far fewer emissions from construction.

Addressing embodied carbon is critically important to lowering overall emissions. As emissions from building operations decrease, the importance of emissions associated with building materials increases. The only emissions generated by zero-carbon buildings are those from their building materials. And once those buildings are built, those emissions are spent: we can do nothing to reduce them. The UN predicts that under a business-as-usual scenario, embodied carbon will represent 49 per cent of global emissions from buildings built between 2020 and 2050 (see Figure 4.2).

Emissions from embodied carbon are not typically included in the carbon accounting for buildings. But if we are to achieve global emissions reductions sufficient to limit global temperature rise to safe levels, we cannot afford to ignore them. The accounting for embodied carbon contained in Vancouver's climate-mitigation plan creates a useful precedent that will allow other cities to follow suit.

Best Practice Examples

There are significant examples of success when architects and engineers think creatively. Brock Commons Tallwood House is an eighteen-story residence at the University of British Columbia in Vancouver. Most of the residence's structural features were built with engineered mass timber instead of concrete. Engineered mass timber uses layers of wood glued or fastened together to form

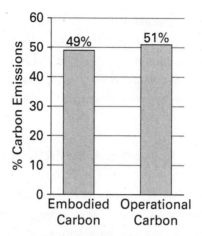

Figure 4.2: Total Carbon Emissions from Global New Construction, 2020–2050 – Business-as-Usual Projection
Source: Based on data from UN Environment, Global Status Report 2017 *and EIA,* International Energy Outlook 2017.

prefabricated strong and stable joists, floors, and outer walls. Only the stairwells and main floor are made with concrete. Estimates put the embodied-carbon savings for the building over conventional construction at 2,432 metric tons of carbon dioxide: the equivalent to emissions from five hundred cars in a year. Tests showed that the residence meets all building-code requirements, including structural performance, fire prevention, and vibration levels. Not only is this the world's tallest timber structure to date, but it has a very low embodied-carbon footprint, it cost less to build, and it was assembled in less than ten weeks.

On the Climate Front Lines

Anyone who has visited China can testify to the incredibly rapid pace of change in that country. Shanghai, for example, is growing so rapidly that a traveler visiting the city twice only a few months apart might not recognize the surroundings. It is often seen as easy to question China's response to climate change, but the government has encouraged a number of cities to create innovative policies to address greenhouse gas emissions. And part of this work is in buildings – Chinese cities are methodically and practically studying best practices from leading western cities to ensure that they begin to adopt world-standard low- or zero-emission building codes.

New York City: New Buildings

New York City is expected to contain eighty thousand to one hundred thousand new buildings by 2050, a huge number. Achieving net zero emissions for the city by 2050 means that these buildings must be constructed to the highest feasible standards, or New York will not meet the goals that science suggests are necessary. To achieve these goals, the city is requiring that all new buildings be net zero carbon by 2030.

Green Building Codes

As noted above, cities differ in their ability to affect changes to building codes. The State of New York allows municipalities to adopt their own building and energy codes, so long as their standards are tougher than those set by the state. Consequently, in 2009, the City of New York began implementing its own building and energy codes.

Until recently, the New York City approach has been to incrementally increase the energy-efficiency requirements for new buildings based on national and international recommendations. These adjustments tended to consider parts of the building independently of the other parts and systems, and are easier to implement from both an industry and regulatory perspective, but possibly miss some benefits that a unified approach would provide. New York has been successful using this framework – for example, in 2016, NYC required air-leakage testing for all new buildings, giving a performance metric for how well the building is air sealed and pointing to where improvements can be made. Plans for future codes include increasing the required levels of insulation for residential buildings – a move projected to reduce total energy use by 25 per cent. These incremental improvements were successful in improving the quality of new buildings in New York, but the city has now recognized that a systemic approach is needed to achieve the energy efficiency required to make net zero carbon cost effective and accessible.

Buildings are far more than the sum of their parts. The energy performance of a building very much depends on how well different systems work together. A frame wall with four inches of insulation, for example, is interrupted every few feet by studs that conduct heat (or cold) past the insulation. If there is a vent going through that wall, from a kitchen fan for example, that vent will also conduct heat (or cold) past the insulation and may introduce leaks to the outside. The net effect is a wall that performs far less efficiently than you'd anticipate from the required four inches of insulation.

New York is therefore taking a new, whole-building approach to its building codes. It is looking at how the different systems work together: the insulation, the structure, the heating and cooling systems, the ventilation systems, the hot-water systems – everything that affects a building's energy efficiency. Starting in 2019, the city is looking to phase in whole-building energy-performance standards, rather than using prescriptive standards that regulate each system independently. The result should be well-insulated buildings with minimal air leakage. These buildings will require relatively little energy to heat, cool, and ventilate, and will therefore require much smaller – and cheaper – heating and cooling systems. This reduces both construction and operational costs: requiring new buildings to be very energy efficient makes sense economically, socially, and climate-wise too.

These changes to the building codes used best practices from national and international organizations, and were developed from the input of thousands of stakeholders through meetings and engagement exercises. Urban Green, a nonprofit organization affiliated with the World Green Building Council, was set up in 2002 to help transform New York City buildings for a sustainable future, and they have been actively involved in engaging stakeholders and making recommendations to the city. A codes advisory committee is also being established to develop the whole-building energy-performance standards to be used in future building codes. Engaging stakeholders early means greater buy-in for changes over the long term.

Leading by Example – Again

During a transformation like this, a city government must demonstrate leadership in its own operations – both for credibility and as a way to show that the changes requested are technically and financially feasible. The City of New York has therefore been investing in significant improvements in the way public buildings are constructed and in reducing the energy use and carbon footprint of their new buildings. Since 2016, new municipal facilities have been required to be constructed so that they use no more than half the operational energy of buildings built to existing standards. This measure demonstrated that constructing buildings to high energy performance was possible and also helped architects, engineers, and tradespeople develop the knowledge and skills necessary for designing and constructing buildings to meet such standards.

In addition, New York City intends to source all electricity for municipal operations from clean sources. Being the biggest energy customer in the city, its demand for clean energy is likely to help transform the system, paving the way to greater installation and adoption of renewable energy by others.

The use of easily available renewable energy helps to expedite the transition to ensure that all new buildings in a city can be net zero carbon. There are currently several options for renewable energy in New York City. Green-power credits are available in the city and are based on electricity generated from renewable sources either within the city or from sources that feed directly into it. These are considered 100 per cent local renewable-energy sources. In addition, the city and the state provide incentives and tax breaks for installation of onsite solar power, and the city is planning to ensure widespread potential for the addition of solar systems to roofs.

This plan doesn't just apply to large buildings. Single-family and semi-detached homes with solar potential are part of a program to require solar readiness. This may mean designing a roof for solar orientation and extra load capacity, installing the necessary wiring and meters for solar arrays, and strategically placing vents, pipes, and other roof-mounted utilities so they will not obstruct an added solar array. Once solar arrays become more affordable – or energy-performance targets get tougher – homeowners could easily add solar arrays to their homes. These buildings could then become net zero carbon.

The Kathleen Grimm School

The Kathleen Grimm School on Staten Island, which opened in 2015, is an inspiring example of how design thinking and use of space can make net zero carbon buildings possible. The school was designed as a pilot project to explore the feasibility of building a school to be net zero carbon (in a climate that has cold winters) and also net zero energy. This means that the school generates, on average, as much electricity from its onsite solar panels as it uses in a year for all its energy needs. The project stretched the imagination of architects, engineers, and even teachers and students.

The first challenge was to design the school to use vastly less energy than a typical school in New York City. This was necessary to ensure that the output from onsite solar panels could match the energy use of the school. Architects and engineers paid careful attention to the siting of the building, the pitch of the roof, the quantity of insulation, and the building's airtightness. Geothermal heat pumps were used for heating and cooling. Special measures were introduced to minimize air leaks, including thirty-foot-tall precast concrete panels on the façade that were designed to curtail punctures to the structure when mounted. Lighting was another important design feature: careful placement of windows allowed classrooms to forgo the use of electric lights up to 90 per cent of the time, and in hallways 98 per cent of the light in daytime comes from windows.

Project-design meetings for the school included consultants, tradespeople, school administrators, faculty, and students – all could discuss how to save energy in every aspect of the school's operation. Even the kitchen consultants found ways to slash energy use by using induction cookers and by rethinking meal planning. The outcome was a school designed to use half the energy of a typical New York City school.

To help create all the projected energy used to heat, cool, and operate the school, solar was chosen – requiring a huge number of solar panels. During the design process, concerns arose that even with solar panels on the roof, on its south-facing walls, and over its parking lot, the energy output of the solar panels would be insufficient to match the building's needs. Accordingly, through a partnership with the Rensselaer Polytechnic Institute (an engineering university in New York State), the solar panels' configuration was optimized to create a projected 35 per cent increased energy output. Thanks to the willingness of the school board, the architects, engineers, and others to try innovative approaches, a public school was built that will generate zero greenhouse gas emissions – all on a constrained municipal budget.

With time, lessons will be learned, expectations will change, and New York City's buildings will become even more energy efficient. It's exciting to think about how the city will look and feel with these carefully designed towers, offices, and homes.

What We See Today

Glass-façade buildings are common in large cities, particularly New York. Such buildings are popular since they are visually appealing, and they're quick and cheap to build. But they're not cheap to operate. Even high-performance glass is a poor insulator. Not only does this mean more energy is needed for heating and cooling, but it can also mean that both heating and cooling are required simultaneously in different parts of the building to keep temperatures stable on a cold, sunny day. This is very energy inefficient. While the new climate-action plan for New York City does not explicitly ban the construction of such buildings, it's clear from the mayor's words and from the performance requirements in the plan that these buildings will be very unlikely to be built in future – meaning that new skyscrapers are likely to look very different and be far more energy efficient.

"We are going to introduce legislation to ban the glass-and-steel skyscrapers that have contributed so much to global warming. They have no place in our city or on our Earth anymore ... If a company wants to build a big skyscraper, they can use a lot of glass if they do all the other things needed to reduce the emissions. But putting up monuments to themselves that harmed our Earth and threatened our future, that will no longer be allowed in New York City."

– Bill de Blasio (New York City), 2019

The Final Word

As South Africa, New York City, and Vancouver have demonstrated, we have all the knowledge, technology, and other tools we need to build emission-free homes, high-rises, and commercial and other buildings. It's often argued that we need to wait to reduce emissions, that it costs too much, or that we need to invent new technologies. It's clear that emissions from buildings are a significant and critical part of emissions in cities – which, as we know, make up about 70 per cent of global emissions. It's also clear that we have the technology today to build affordable buildings that generate zero or near-zero emissions – as we've seen with Tallwood House at UBC and the Kathleen Grimm School in New York. Programs such as Vancouver's assist the construction industry in developing better materials, technologies, and techniques – all of which aid in the transformation we need. But that transformation doesn't depend on those advanced technologies – it can be, and is being, done today. What it does depend on is political will. With that, in cities around the world, these steps can be duplicated if decision makers accept the value and viability of net-zero-carbon buildings with low embodied carbon – and people demand it. They can demand it with their voices, their votes – and their wallets. People choosing to buy energy-efficient buildings would ensure the market adapted rapidly, even in places where leadership from the city government is absent. Given the far lower costs of ownership, their wallets would benefit, too.

Chapter 5

Public Transportation

London's underground map is so iconic that it adorns T-shirts of youth worldwide. Paris, Berlin, New York, Chicago, Tokyo – all cities with significant rail-based mass transit that serves their residents well and that can support the kind of density necessary to create environmentally and economically efficient cities. These cities, each with excellent subway systems, show how much public transportation matters – to meeting the transportation needs of residents, to the city's economic success, to air quality, to equity and inclusivity. Transportation also matters very much to climate change. It is a critical source of greenhouse gas emissions, particularly in cities. Typically, dense, built-up cities with excellent public transit systems tend to be places where relatively more people take transit and fewer drive – and consequently, greenhouse gas emissions are lower.

But subways are not the only way to successfully move vast numbers of people quickly and efficiently – a lesson from Curitiba, Brazil.

Curitiba is a city of nearly two million people in the south of Brazil and is the capital of the state of Paraná. Not nearly as well known to those outside Brazil as Rio de Janeiro or Sao Paulo, it is nonetheless important economically and socially. It is home to the University of Paraná, to significant manufacturing and food processing, and to industries such as paper and wood processing. At least since 1940, the economy of Curitiba has been strong and growing, powered by both external and internal migration – so much that more than half of its current residents were not born in the city.

It has also been home to a visionary and effective mayor, Jaime Lerner, who was mayor for three separate terms between 1971 and 1992, and then governor of the state for two more. Mayor Lerner is known for building new parks and lakes, for making the city center walkable, for a strong belief in equity – and among those who study public transportation, for the revolution in public transportation he introduced in his third term as mayor. Not by subway, but by bus.

**

Dense Cities Are Good for the Environment

How does a city need to be built? From an environmental perspective, and increasingly from an economic-efficiency and social-inclusion perspective, cities are trying to make themselves places where residents can live without having to own a car. In the longer term, it is possible to build cities that promote transit use and active transportation – walking and cycling – over driving. We see this in cities as varied as New York, Tokyo, and Copenhagen, where density (in the cases of New York and Tokyo) or effective planning (in the case of Copenhagen) have resulted in cities with high rates of transit ridership, walking, and cycling. In these, and similar cities, statistics (known as modal share) show that residents favor transit or active transportation. They demonstrate that it is possible to build cities that meet the transportation needs of all residents, while helping to create healthier places to live. Of the people who live and work in Manhattan, only 5 per cent drive to work – 42 per cent take the subway or bus, and the majority walk, ride, take a taxi, or do something else. In Copenhagen, the split in favor of active transportation is even more dramatic – more than 40 per cent of residents commute by bicycle.

There is a popular image that shows how much space is taken up by sixty people occupying individual cars versus the considerably smaller space taken up by those same sixty people contained in a bus or on bicycles. That comparison demonstrates one reason for the success of transit, walking, and cycling matter: using limited space in cities for active transportation is far more efficient than any alternatives – and public transportation is far more efficient than cars.

The gold standard in public transportation can be found in cities such as Tokyo, Berlin, and New York, where density and history have combined to create networks of regional rail, subways, streetcars, and buses that enable virtually anyone to access reliable, inexpensive, and quick public transport. Particularly when powered by clean electricity grids, rail-based transit is highly advantageous from an environmental perspective. Build it (a network), and they will come – out of their cars and onto transit.

Transit networks have other advantages for cities. They make dense urban development possible and – given that economic studies clearly show that dense urban environments are more productive – help to create jobs and prosperity. They help address inequality, by not requiring people to own and pay for expensive vehicles to participate in social and economic life. They help to address air quality and other local health issues – and, of course, they help to lower greenhouse gas emissions.

New Rail-Based Rapid Transit in Unlikely Places

Cities in Europe such as Berlin and Paris long ago built excellent rail, metro, tram (light rail transit), and bus networks that allow people to live far more sustainable lives because they do not have to use a car to partake of the life of the city. This is true elsewhere – such as New York and Tokyo, Chicago and Toronto, Montreal and Milan. All these cities have benefitted economically too, as the density possible from permanent rail transit has helped create significant wealth over time. It would benefit many other cities if they built subways and light rail transit (LRT) – and we know that's possible, from examples as varied as Los Angeles and Addis Ababa.

Los Angeles

Today we can see exciting examples of cities building more public transport to help residents more easily choose rapid transit. In the County of Los Angeles (which includes the city and surrounding region), nearly 70 per cent of residents voted for Measure M in 2016, a sales tax increase ballot proposition with substantial funding for transit projects, walking, and cycling. The funds will allow for a significant increase in subway and light rail lines and additional busways to create a massive expansion to the region's network. In a city noted for its devotion to cars, it is telling that a tax increase to fund transit and active transportation so overwhelmingly passed. And the City of Los Angeles plans to ensure that significant portions of this work are fully complete by 2028 – in time for the LA Olympic Games.

Addis Ababa

The East African country of Ethiopia is located in a hilly region just west of the Horn of Africa. Its capital, Addis Ababa, is a modern metropolitan city with a population of more than three million inhabitants and rising fast: by 2037 it is projected to be ten million. It is dubbed the political capital of Africa as many international organizations are headquartered there, including the African Union and the United Nations Economic Commission for Africa. Addis

Ababa struggles with high poverty rates, large informal settlements, and other challenges common to major African cities.

As of 2016, transportation was responsible for nearly half of the city's greenhouse gas emissions. On a global scale the city's emissions are relatively low – the average European city creates sixty times the amount of emissions. But Addis Ababa does not want to create a problem as it grows and is looking to manage greenhouse gas emissions well. For economic as well as environmental reasons, the city is planning to become more compact and connected. Its plans include a commitment to transit-oriented development – building around and near transit lines and stations.

Addis Ababa's population currently gets around largely by foot. Roughly 60 per cent of residents walk to their destinations. As the city grows, incomes increase, and livelihoods change, residents will probably increasingly seek other ways to get around. That means more transportation infrastructure and, if based on the automobile, more congestion and more emissions. Roads are congested today, and the vehicles are older and highly polluting.

An efficient and affordable public transportation system is essential for Addis Ababa's social and economic development. As the city's population grows, the poorest find themselves at the edge of the city, where lack of transportation options means lack of access to jobs and opportunities for socioeconomic mobility. For these and other reasons, in 2015 Addis Ababa became the first sub-Saharan African city to develop an LRT system. (LRT systems are rail-based electric transit systems that have their own right of way and typically use European-style tram technology, rather than "heavy rail" – larger and heavier vehicles used in subways.) The two-line system carries up to sixty thousand passengers per hour and regularly reaches full capacity. In a congested city where road traffic travels at an average speed of ten kilometers per hour (about 6 miles per hour), the LRT is a welcome alternative with average speeds of twenty-two kilometers per hour (about 13 to 14 miles per hour).

Ethiopia's electricity comes almost exclusively from hydro-power. As a result, this system has zero operational emissions. In 2015, the city's calculations showed that the LRT in Addis Ababa

Modern, sleek, and effective light rail in Addis Ababa – like an above-ground subway. Source: Goddard_Photography/iStockphoto.com.

eliminated significant amounts of carbon dioxide (55 kilotons), a value projected to grow to 170 per year by 2030.

The LRT is indeed helping to develop a more compact and connected city. Areas close to LRT stations are seeing increased development. In some areas of the city, buildings are being torn down, and new, taller buildings are taking their place. The condominiums and multifamily housing that are appearing allow for far greater population densities, but as in western cities, there is a risk that the lowest-income inhabitants cannot afford this new housing and will need to live farther and farther from the city center, a consequence that would be explicitly contrary to the intent of the proponents of these changes.

The LRT system was largely paid for with concession loans from the Export-Import Bank of China. Operation and maintenance responsibilities were shared between Ethiopian and Chinese companies. Ethiopian workers were trained to operate and manage the LRT and gradually took over full management of the system.

The financing has been a challenge – repaying loans while keeping fares low is a difficult juggling act – but ridership is very high:

clear evidence of a need for clean electric mass transit in a large developing city.

From a climate perspective, we don't have to wait for cities to find the resources and leadership to massively expand subways and light rail – there are numerous steps that can be taken in the short term that make a very real difference in providing better transit and lowering emissions immediately. Building or expanding a network as Los Angeles is doing will take time – which gives rise to a question: How can public transport be used to dramatically lower greenhouse gas emissions in the short term, as we plan and build the networks our cities and their residents need in the longer term?

> *"The first article in every constitution in the world says that all citizens are equal before the law. This may sound like a nicety, but it is actually a very powerful statement. Because if citizens are equal before the law, a bus with 100 or 150 passengers should have the right to 150 times more road space than a car with one person."*
>
> **– Mayor Enrique Peñalosa (Bogota),**
> **International Transport Forum, 2011**

Frugal and Effective: Bus Rapid Transit

The answer is the bus – sometimes considered the lowly bus. But buses are a critical part of the transportation solution for global cities. In 2017, it was estimated that there were approximately three million buses in municipal fleets across the world. To meet urban transport needs and address climate challenges, we need more – and better – buses. Bus rapid transit powered by clean electric buses has the power to both increase the relative use of transit in a city and to dramatically reduce greenhouse gas emissions from transit. McKinsey tells us that greenhouse gases can be reduced by these advances – up to 25 per cent – advances that are feasible in most world cities today at relatively low cost and that are quickly achievable, in line with the urgency needed to act on the climate crisis.

Under the leadership of Mayor Lerner, in the 1970s the City of Curitiba took a bold step to address its transportation challenges. At that time Curitiba was in the midst of a growth spurt that continues to this day, and the rapid population expansion had driven planners at the state level to suggest solutions that were popular at the time – more and wider roads, and subways underneath. Mayor Lerner, an architect by profession, saw things differently.

> *"A system of bus rapid transit is not only dedicated lanes. You have to have really good boarding conditions – that means paying before entering the bus and boarding at the same level. And at the same time having a good schedule and frequency."*
>
> **– Mayor Jaime Lerner (Curitiba), 2011**

He saw potential in the bus and designed a system that used the advantages of rail systems – permanent infrastructure and its own right of way – but integrated this infrastructure along the city's main arteries. This allowed the buses to operate at speeds similar to light rail, at a fraction of the cost, and – equally importantly – allowed the system to be built in a fraction of the time it would have taken to build a subway system. Gradually, the bus system became

The easy boarding system that helped transform Curitiba by turning a bus into rapid transit. Note how the doors facilitate easy loading and unloading, making the service efficient and effective. Source: tupungato/iStockphoto.com.

highly successful, carrying huge ridership (more than 2.4 million people, as of the latest available ridership figures).

In 1991, in his third term as mayor, Lerner added a distinctive feature designed to dramatically lower boarding times and thereby improve service – new tube-like stations where riders pay before they board. The stations also allow for access to the buses for riders with mobility difficulties, including those in wheelchairs. With the addition of these new stations, buses were able to provide exceptional service – on some routes, there is a bus every ninety seconds. Many give the mayor credit for creating the first bus rapid transit (BRT) system in the world.

This idea has proven to be successful. Bogota, the capital of Colombia and a busy city with its own historical challenges, decided to build a BRT (the TransMilenio) based on Curitiba's system. The city argued that a full system could be designed and built at about the cost of one short subway line, and in 2001 the Bogota BRT was opened. Like Curitiba, passengers board from raised platforms and pay before boarding. The system is accessible for people with wheelchairs and has both express and local services. As was the case in Curitiba, routes were planned to spur prosperity in economically deprived neighborhoods. The city also measures air quality, randomly testing buses each day to ensure standards are met.

This movement is not restricted to South America – Addis Ababa itself is also adding a BRT system to complement the LRT. One sixteen-kilometer (ten-mile) corridor is under development, and six others are planned for development by 2030. This system is expected to be faster, more comfortable, safer, more reliable, more accessible for those with physical challenges, and produce lower levels of emissions relative to the minibuses that are used now.

In Addis Ababa, early and extensive public and stakeholder consultations were essential to help the city understand possible impacts of the changes and to help residents plan for and embrace the new LRT and BRT systems. Drivers and owners of the minibuses whose routes will be displaced by the new BRT system, for example, have legitimate concerns about loss of income and livelihoods. The city has therefore been working to employ displaced workers in its BRT system and to offer shareholder positions in the bus-operating company to minibus operators.

Addis Ababa carried out extensive research on LRT and BRT systems in other cities before embarking on its own projects. Learning from the experience of others allowed the city to avoid a number of the pitfalls and obstacles that other cities have encountered. A dismantled BRT system in Delhi, for example, showed the need for properly designed terminals and coordinated marketing and information campaigns. As Addis Ababa rolls out its own BRT, the system will itself become a model and learning opportunity for other developing cities. Indeed, C40 Cities predicts that the public transportation system will be a "blueprint for local expansion and regional replication." As the first LRT plus BRT in sub-Saharan Africa, the system in Addis Ababa sets an exceptionally important precedent for other African cities for how to build transit that provides personal mobility without reliance on the automobile and its related pollution.

Buy More Buses

We need more buses if we are to move people efficiently to where they need to go – buses are cheap and effective. Often an increase in bus service in a built-up city – or a small town – can be accomplished when other projects would take significant time due to cost and complexity. For example, between 2003 and 2010 Toronto adopted a strategy focused on increased bus service and better value (allowing the unlimited-use pass then named the Metropass to be used by multiple family members) to dramatically increase transit ridership.

Toronto is a large built-up city of nearly three million people in the heart of an urban region of about six million. While it has a built-up and dense urban core reminiscent of Chicago or Manhattan, it's also a city with a spread-out set of inner suburbs designed not for transit but for the car. While the city has an excellent transit service, the Toronto Transit Commission (TTC), its core rapid transit – subway and streetcar – is really designed to serve a city of half the size. Over time, while new rapid transit projects are being built, significant practical reliance on buses continues. Some of Toronto's bus routes are exceptionally busy – for example, the Finch West bus route that serves the northwest inner suburbs of the city has more than forty thousand riders a day, making it one of the busiest transit routes in North America. To give some perspective, that's about 25 per cent of the entire ridership of Boston's Green Line light rail/subway system.

In 2003 and 2004 the TTC recognized the potential of improved bus service by adopting and implementing the Ridership Growth Strategy. A commitment was made to riders that there would be bus service within one hundred meters (about 110 yards) of every residence, and at least fifteen-minute service on all routes until 2 a.m. Service on the existing network of night buses and streetcars was improved, and new routes added to ensure reasonable twenty-four-hour access to bus service citywide. This drove significant ridership gains, as shown in Figure 5.1.

Toronto's efforts show the potential for simple measures to make a large difference in growing ridership for public transit, thereby

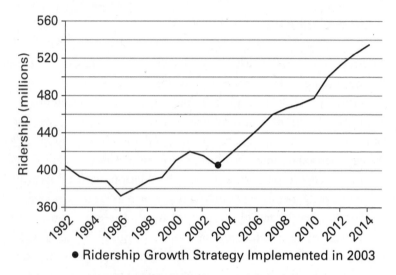

● Ridership Growth Strategy Implemented in 2003

Figure 5.1: TTC Annual Ridership, 1992–2014
Toronto showed that simple strategies can drive significant ridership growth.
Source: Based on data from Toronto Transit Commission, 2016.

achieving better environmental results – but was instituted at a time when buses were predominantly diesel or hybrid. We now know that it is also possible for the buses themselves to be a much bigger part of the climate solution.

Clean the Air

Air pollution is a serious global health issue. The World Health Organization (WHO) estimates that there are 4.2 million premature deaths every year from outdoor air pollution. And most of us are exposed: more than 90 per cent of the world's population lives in areas where the air quality fails to meet WHO standards.

Historically, most buses are powered with diesel, a particularly dirty fuel. Diesel vehicles are a major contributor to bad air quality. These engines emit fine particulate matter, smog-forming compounds, nitrogen oxides, sulfur dioxide, and other toxic substances. Diesel exhaust can deposit soot deep in our lungs, irritate our respiratory systems, weaken our immune systems, and some exhaust compounds have been linked to cancer. Fetuses, young children, and those with chronic illnesses are particularly vulnerable.

Electric buses produce none of these tailpipe emissions. Even when the electricity used to power electric buses is generated from coal, the buses typically are responsible for producing fewer greenhouse gas emissions and less pollution than diesel buses: power plants are built with pollution-control measures not found on buses.

For almost every city, the pathway to zero-carbon public transportation involves electric buses. Electric buses can be added to the city's public transportation system quickly and easily, because other than charging infrastructure, which can be concentrated in centralized facilities, they require no additional land, construction, or municipal redevelopment. And when the electricity used to power the buses is zero carbon, so too are the buses. But until very recently, electric buses were seen as only possible in the future. Today, except for cities in difficult climates where battery performance is still being assessed, electric buses are here, are reliable, and have been proven in enough cities that a rapid transition can happen now.

In most cities, barriers to adoption of clean electric buses are not technical but financial – even though the lifetime cost is lower, they are more expensive to buy, and that creates an obstacle in many places. Although electric buses are currently more expensive to buy than their diesel counterparts they have lower operating costs: today, in a busy transit system, they have a lower lifetime cost than diesel (due to the lower maintenance costs), and they are projected by Bloomberg New Energy Finance to have purchase price parity with diesels by 2030.

Numerous cities have made a strong commitment to electric buses. They have demonstrated that the real obstacle to dramatically reducing emissions from the world's bus fleets is inertia.

On the Climate Front Lines

Kolkata, India (formerly Calcutta), capital city of West Bengal State in India, is a city of about 4.5 million people, in the heart of an urban region of more than 14 million. It is a globally significant city with a noteworthy cultural, commercial, and educational history, and currently is the third-largest city economy in the country. Like most of India, Kolkata's electricity is generated from coal-fired power plants, causing significant air-quality issues. As would be expected, its transportation systems are exceptionally busy. Positive transportation measures have a great impact on social, economic, and environmental life. Public transport is critical — nearly 90 per cent of all trips are on public transport. In this context, clean, nonpolluting vehicles are important to ensure clearer air, lower greenhouse gas emissions, and a continuing willingness of residents to use the public system. The West Bengal State government therefore has decided to fund a transition of the entire bus and ferry fleet to electric over the next decade, starting with 180 electric buses by the end of 2020. These buses alone will eliminate more than fourteen thousand metric tons of CO_2 – and reduce operating costs, by up to two-thirds.

Better, Cleaner Buses: From China to the World

China is often thought to be a climate laggard but is actually a leader in electric transportation. Shenzhen, a city of nearly thirteen million permanent residents, has nine hundred bus lines, and more than sixteen thousand buses, all of which are electric (Figure 5.2). It has the world's first 100 per cent electric bus fleet, which it created in little more than six years (starting in 2011).

Conversion to a fully electric fleet of buses reduced Shenzhen's greenhouse gas emissions by an estimated 1.35 million tons per year. Even though the electricity that powers these buses is largely generated from fossil fuels, the power plants have stronger pollution control measures than those available for diesel vehicles.

The buses are capable of traveling an average of 250 kilometers (about 155 miles) on a charge. A full recharge takes five hours, so most bus routes have charging facilities. The city currently operates

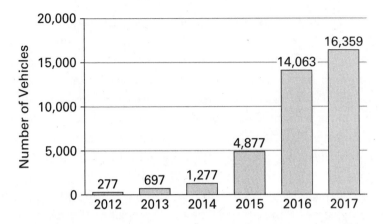

Figure 5.2: Electric Bus Adoption in Shenzhen, China, 2012–2017
Shenzhen implemented an entirely electric bus fleet in an extraordinarily short time. Source: Based on data from Shenzhen Urban Transport Planning and Design Institute Co. Ltd.

one charging outlet for every three electric buses, and some of these stations double as charge points for private cars and taxis.

The city government also is driving electric bus adoption as an economic development strategy. BYD (which stands for "Build Your Dreams"), a global leader in manufacturing electric buses, supplied nearly all of Shenzhen's buses and is headquartered there, employing forty thousand people.

As of 2017, 99 per cent of the world's 385,000 electric buses could be found in China, partly because of important subsidies provided by the national government that lowered the cost of acquisition and provided a direct stimulus to the emerging manufacturing industry. Until 2016, more than half the costs of a new electric bus were covered by these subsidies, making them the most cost-effective option for Chinese cities. Now that the cost of new buses is rapidly dropping as a result of advances in manufacturing and the growth of the industry, the Chinese government is phasing out the subsidies, which will disappear completely by 2021. The program demonstrates how smart policies can drive positive change, make cities better places to live – and create jobs.

Electric Bus Adoption Can Spread Rapidly

It isn't essential, however, to have the support of a powerful central-ized government to convert a fleet to electric buses. Santiago, Chile, has also made wonderful progress on its electric bus rollout – and it has done so without major federal subsidies.

Santiago is located in a valley between two mountain ranges. As a consequence, pollution becomes trapped in the valley, particularly in the winter months when the cold air pools in low-lying areas, allowing pollution levels to build up. This has health and economic consequences for the city: four thousand premature deaths per year are attributed to air pollution, and the annual health care costs of this problem amount to more than US$500 million – recent figures suggest as much as US$670 million.

In the winter months, it is not uncommon for the city to declare environmental emergencies due to harmful concentrations of smog. On these days, polluting industries are forced to shut down their operations, a significant percentage of cars are banned from city roads (based on license plate numbers), the use of home wood-stoves is prohibited, and people are encouraged to stay indoors. This has economic and social repercussions that have caused citizens to demand that government address air quality. As expected, the course of action that reduces air pollution also reduces greenhouse gas emissions.

In 2012, 79 per cent of Santiago's greenhouse gas emissions came from transportation, while 38 per cent of all trips in the city were made using public transportation. The city needed a way to reduce the pollution and emissions generated from their public transit to help mitigate the air-quality challenges. Electric buses were an important part of the solution.

In 2017, Santiago took an important step toward electrifying its bus fleet by starting a pilot program with two electric buses leased from the local affiliate of BYD – Enel-BYD. It added a further 200 electric buses between December 2018 and the end of January 2019, and in October of 2019, it took possession of 180 more, well on its way to achieving its goal of converting 25 per cent of its roughly

6,600 buses to electric by 2025. And by 2040, Santiago aims to have an all-electric fleet.

It is important to understand how remarkable it is to add nearly four hundred electric buses in less than a year. Fleet purchases – buses, garbage trucks, postal delivery vans – are planned out over many years, sometimes decades. Changing purchasing plans quickly requires decisive leadership. Other cities are studying electric buses, some are piloting, many are debating the costs and merits. Santiago *committed* to electric buses. Today, Santiago has the biggest electric bus fleet in Latin America and one of the biggest fleets globally. Its leadership demonstrates that in South America, it is practical and feasible to make a rapid transition from diesel to electric transportation – an important step in addressing the significant portion of urban greenhouse gas emissions caused by transportation.

The buses that Santiago chose, like those in Shenzhen, are capable of traveling 250 kilometers (155 miles) per charge. This means that, despite steep roads and heavy ridership, these buses are capable of completing their entire daily route on a single charge with recharging occurring at night. Two depots at opposite ends of the city have been upgraded to accommodate charging for the buses, and at the time of writing this book, three new charging depots were under construction.

Those charging depots have double duty. Solar panels covering the parking areas provide some of the energy used to power these buses. Some buses are served by a contract that ensures the power used for their charging is sourced from 100 per cent certified renewable energy.

Santiago is one of the cities that is taking advantage of innovative financing options for its electric buses. A "turnkey" lease model is used here. Two energy service companies (Engie and Enel X) supply all the services required to operate electric buses in the city: the buses, the charging infrastructure, the maintenance services, and the energy used to power the buses. This lease agreement is part of an overall partnership between the manufacturer of the buses, the energy service companies, the municipal bus operators, and the Chilean government.

According to media reports, transit riders are enthusiastic about the electric buses. The buses are new, cleaner, quiet and have a smoother ride, and also come with perks. These include air conditioning, free Wi-Fi, USB chargers – and no smell of diesel. Rather than arrive at work stressed from traffic, Santiago's electric bus riders can relax, play games, or even work as they travel to their destination.

Santiago has also adopted city-planning measures to complement the use of public transit through active transportation. To help transit users get to their destinations faster and easier, the city has introduced bus-only lanes and bus-signal priority. The city center was redesigned to give priority to active- and public-transportation users, including adding cycling infrastructure, a bikeshare program with 2,600 bikes, a free bicycle taxi in the city center, and cycling education in primary schools.

Electric buses are viable in European and North American contexts as well. Milan, which is a city where electrified transit has a long history, has demonstrated what is possible.

Building on History in Italy

Milan is a modern, business city – but a city with roots going back to the fourth century BCE. Its tram system was introduced in 1876 and still forms a critical part of the public transportation system today. Although the first trams were pulled by horses, the system was fully electrified by 1901 and remains electric to this day. Some of the earliest trams, introduced to the city between 1928 and 1930, are still in operation. (These iconic trains are similar to those that operated in a number of North American cities such as San Francisco and are an early example of how transformative ideas can spread rapidly from city to city.) In total, Milan currently has nineteen tram lines with 175 kilometers (about 109 miles) of tracks. Like a spider's web, most of these tracks radiate out from the city center, connecting the suburbs to the downtown.

Milan also has a network of trolley buses. These electric buses source their energy from overhead lines like trams, but unlike trams, they do not require tracks embedded in the road. Trolley buses were introduced in 1933 and remain a vital part of Milan's public transportation network, primarily moving passengers around Milan's outer ring road. The latest versions are equipped with batteries that allow the buses to travel up to fifteen kilometers (about nine miles) off the overhead network, which gives the buses the ability to detour around construction, accidents, and other road obstacles.

Milan also has four extensive subway lines extending one hundred kilometers (about 62 miles), and a fifth is under construction.

The last component of Milan's public transportation system is its buses. Its 1,502 buses are nearly all diesel powered, and they are the major target for electrification. By 2030, Milan plans to convert its entire bus fleet to electric; at that point, it will be the first major European city to have a fully electric transportation system: trams, trolleys, subways, and buses.

Milan is building the infrastructure needed to support a fully electric bus fleet. Four new bus depots with automated recharging are planned, with the first to be completed in 2021. In addition, three bus depots are being restructured to accommodate the needs of electric buses. On-route charging will also be available at termi-nuses across the city.

As it waits for the charging infrastructure to be built, Milan is replacing its oldest buses with hybrid electric buses. These buses have an electric motor that is recharged through regenerative brak-ing and an internal combustion engine, and they emit up to 30 per cent less carbon dioxide pollution than their full-diesel counter-parts. Some models are designed to use the electric motor exclu-sively when stopping and starting to reduce the air pollution levels around the bus stops where people congregate.

The electricity that powers the trams, the trolley buses, the sub-way trains, and soon the buses is 100 per cent renewable. Once the last diesel bus is gone in 2030, Milan will have a zero-emissions pub-lic transportation system. Promotion of the use of public transporta-tion is therefore a critical strategy for the success of its climate-action plan. Located near the car-manufacturing centers of Italy, Milan has one of the highest rates of personal-vehicle ownership in Europe.

However, ridership of the public transportation system is also high. More than two million trips per day are taken on the system within a metropolitan area with slightly more than eight million inhabitants.

To help provide alternatives to personal vehicle use, Milan offers additional services. Many of its bus routes operate all night, and in some districts, an on-demand "radio bus" is available to get you to your final destination late at night. Parking is available near transit routes, and there is a bikeshare program connected to transit that includes e-bikes and even child seats.

The Final Word

Zero-emission public transportation is possible today. Many cities have excellent subway systems, light rail, or streetcars. Those need to be expanded both for transportation reasons and so the city can grow in a dense and sustainable way. At the same time, decarbonizing a significant part of the public transportation system is possible – in the very short term – by transitioning rapidly to quiet, clean, electric buses.

While China has made the most progress, it's clear from other global cities that electric buses are viable now and result in significant improvements to air quality, noise, and carbon emissions. Smart governments are using the right public transport policy to create jobs and new industries supplying those buses. Santiago shows that this model works in South America, and Milan demonstrates how a multi-modal public transportation system can also become zero carbon in Europe. Addis Ababa, a city in a developing country in Africa, is moving toward zero-emission public transportation. It is clear from these examples that there are no technical impediments to the mass adoption of electric public transport – only inertia and a lack of political will. Zero-emission public transportation protects our climate and our health, keeps our cities clean, helps us move around, and increases the mobility of our most vulnerable. Like most good climate policy, it's a win for all.

Chapter 6

Personal and Other Transportation

In 2009, building on an idea that then mayor Gérald Tremblay learned from the mayor of Paris, Montreal created a new bikeshare program, BIXI. The city's parking authority started a private, non-profit company to build the BIXI bicycles and operate the program. The BIXI bikes (a hybrid of BIcycle and taXI) are designed for heavy use and abuse. Seeing Montreal's success, other cities bought BIXI bikes to use in their bikeshare programs, helping to grow this manufacturing industry in Montreal. The bikeshare program is popular with residents of Montreal: last year, nearly six million bikeshare trips were made. A hit song has even been written about it, "The Bixi Anthem," by hip hop band Da Gryptions.

***

Do an internet image search of "traffic" or "traffic jams" or "congestion" and you'll find images of traffic congestion from almost every major city in the world. You'll see images from Nairobi. Shanghai. Hong Kong. Delhi. And Los Angeles, of course. Images of massive traffic jams in Los Angeles, with its famous congestion on famous highways such as the 405.

This congestion has a variety of causes, but the heart of it is that many cities have been allowed to grow in a spread-out way (urban sprawl) around a transportation system based on the private automobile. As spread-out communities are not built to the densities that support effective and affordable public transit, traveling by car becomes the only real choice for people. Add to this commercial transportation, and the result is a transportation system that does not effectively meet the mobility needs of millions of people, particularly in rush hour.

Interesting work is happening in many automobile-dependent cities to address this challenge. Much of that work – such as municipal policies to encourage future development along transit lines (known as transit-oriented development) – is long term and beyond the scope of this book, which attempts to demonstrate measures being taken now that can be replicated quickly to dramatically reduce emissions. But the scale of the challenge also reveals an opportunity: gas- and diesel-burning cars and trucks produce exhaust, resulting in substantial greenhouse gas emissions (and other air pollution), but changes being made in cities around the world help to meaningfully reduce such emissions – today.

Cities with excellent public transport systems have a smaller climate footprint. The environmental impact of a dense city (as opposed to a spread-out one) is lesser, on a per-person basis, and economically, dense cities are more efficient and productive. People are drawn to such cities by the prospect of a better job, a better life. Ensuring that public transport is easy and convenient for all residents is a crucial part of city building, and powering it by clean electricity can dramatically reduce greenhouse gas emissions. Zero-emission – and comprehensive – public transportation systems are an essential part of the immediate solution for reducing emissions from the transportation system. Dense cities that favor good public transit are also often cities where it is easy to walk, cycle, or use other forms of active transportation. But in the short term, as they improve public transit, many cities need to address how to both reduce personal-vehicle use and how to help citizens make the switch to zero-emission vehicles. At the same time, city governments own or control significant fleets of vehicles themselves. This chapter will show what cities are doing today to address emissions from vehicles and fleets – measures that can be rapidly adopted globally.

Congestion Charging, Low-Emission Zones, and a Comprehensive Approach to Clean Transportation

Question: What can cities do to address emissions from transportation, in a world where many of the policy and regulatory controls – such as the standards to which motor vehicles must be built – are held by federal and other governments? Answer: Cities have a significant ability to influence the adoption of clean transportation systems by using the regulatory powers they do have, by showing leadership in their own fleet operations, and by using the bully pulpit of the mayor. Cities can favor active transportation over the car; they can make low-emission vehicles the preferred choice through smart regulatory and other interventions, and they can use business-licensing requirements creatively to ensure that low-emission vehicles become the norm. Some of these steps require political courage, but there are multiple examples of policies that have initially been bitterly contested becoming popular because they work – and because people want to live in less congested cities with clean air.

London

Cities need to address transportation systems for reasons well beyond climate change, but their efforts can also significantly reduce greenhouse gas emissions. In thinking about transportation, a city needs to consider the decisions that its citizens make every day about how to get to their destinations. To build a low-emission city, emission-free forms of getting around should be the default choice, and for that to happen, those choices must be easy, convenient, affordable, and enjoyable.

For nearly a century, city planning in many places has focused on the car. As a result, making zero-emission transportation the standard requires a rethinking of how infrastructure is designed, how the rules for the use of the road are established, and of how (and by whom) public space is used. Not surprisingly, this rethinking of transportation policies in major cities has been at times controversial. But some cities, concerned about pollution, congestion, and greenhouse gas emissions, have taken bold steps – steps that were controversial at the time of proposal but which have most often proved highly popular once implemented, when residents see the benefits of easier, cleaner transportation choices.

London, England, is a historic city, nearly two thousand years old. It has an excellent public transit network, but by the year 2000 the combination of its narrow streets, dense historical core, and high rates of personal-vehicle use had resulted in major congestion. In addition to traffic problems, this congestion greatly affected air quality, and – of course – caused greenhouse gas emissions.

It has been estimated that thousands of London residents die every year due to air pollution, and that air pollution, including that from vehicular exhaust, is associated with increased rates of asthma, reduced lung capacity, mental health problems, dementia, strokes, and other major health conditions. Children are particularly vulnerable, and in London, hundreds of schools are situated in areas that exceed legal and safe air-pollution levels. This has a considerable social and economic toll on the city.

To address these mobility and public health issues, London undertook years of painstaking research and sought reports from working groups. The research conclusively showed that a charge on vehicles would dramatically reduce the traffic entering the central city – thereby reducing emissions and improving air quality. This idea – known as "congestion charging" – was introduced in 2003 by Mayor

Ken Livingstone. At the time, according to the BBC, it was the "biggest congestion charge scheme ever undertaken by a capital city."

A congestion charge is a daily fee charged to vehicles that drive into or park in congestion-zones during regular business hours. In London, cameras are used to capture license plate numbers throughout the congestion zone, and charges are paid online or through an automatic-payment system. The current daily charge is £11.50 (about US$15) and the zone covers central London – the area within the London inner ring road. Buses, standard taxis, service vehicles, and motorcycles are exempt from congestion charging, and discounts are available for residents and persons with disabilities. Ultra-low-emissions vehicles also qualify for discounts.

Studies have shown that congestion charging reduced the number of cars entering the zone during business hours. In the first year of congestion charging, there were a third fewer cars and minicabs on the streets during business hours. It was estimated that half of the diverted trips by car were switched to trips by bus, which reinforced one of the critical actions taken by Mayor Livingstone at inception. He dramatically increased bus service at exactly the same time as the start of the congestion charge – thereby facilitating transportation choices for those affected. Taxis also saw a significant increase in ridership. And travel delays caused by congestion fell by 30 per cent.

Initially, the congestion-charge proposal was extremely unpopular. Mayor Livingstone withstood significant public challenge, including from his Conservative opponent in the 2004 election, who said that the charge wouldn't work and vowed to cancel both it and any fines for nonpayment. That stance was supported by the Conservative Party and by some sectors of the business community, who claimed that the charges would hurt business. Tony Blair, the Labour prime minister, urged London members of the party to vote against the congestion charge. A legal challenge was brought against it by Westminster City Council on the basis that it breached the human rights of residents, would drive pollution to areas outside the zone, and cut people off from essential services. The case was unsuccessful.

Strategic planning – as London did by increasing alternative transportation options when it introduced the congestion charge – is critical when facilitating a major shift in behaviors and perspectives. Source: cheekylorns/iStockphoto.com.

The critics were wrong. The charge worked. Traffic congestion plummeted. Business was more successful, not less. And Ken Livingstone was reelected.

> *"Retail sales in central London are far outperforming those in the rest of the country. The West End theater trade is strong. Tourism is growing strongly. Congestion charging has achieved exactly what it was designed to do – not cut the number of journeys but shift them from private cars to public transport. It has cut congestion, and cut environmental damage, with the economy continuing to boom."*
>
> **– Mayor Ken Livingstone (London), 2007**

The Conservatives, unfortunately from the perspective of climate action, maintained their position, and Boris Johnson, who defeated Ken Livingstone in 2008, repealed an extension of the zone and prevented rate increases. As a result, congestion has slowly increased in London, eventually reaching pre-2003 levels. Johnson did support, however, the implementation of a low-emission zone (LEZ) to help combat air pollution from transportation sources. The zone covers most of Greater London and operates all day, every day. LEZ charges apply to older diesel heavy vehicles: transport trucks, coaches, utility vehicles, and the like. Designed to incentivize better route planning, upgrades, and fleet renewal, the charges are significant: £300 (approximately US$385) per day in 2020 on top of any other congestion and emission-zone charges. Applicable vehicles can sometimes be fitted with filters or adapted to use less-polluting fuel to avoid paying the charges, but the emissions standards were designed from inception to become stricter over time. Some businesses have reorganized their fleets to reduce deliveries and to use only new vehicles within London, and in some cases, businesses have chosen to retire their older vehicles early to avoid the charges. The result: fewer emissions from the dirtiest vehicles within Greater London.

Under the leadership of the current mayor, Sadiq Khan, London has continued its progress. To reach zero emissions, reduce pollution, and alleviate gridlock the mayor's office has developed a comprehensive transportation strategy with clear goals. By 2050, all vehicles in the city will be zero emission, including personal vehicles, taxis, and buses. By 2041, 80 per cent of trips within the city will be walking, biking, or public transit. Zero-emission zones, places where no fossil fuel powered cars are allowed, will expand from the central city to the entirety of London by 2050.

In 2019, building on the work of Mayor Livingstone and on the LEZ supported by his predecessor, Mayor Kahn introduced the ultra-low-emission zone (ULEZ) – a measure explicitly designed to address air quality and climate change. The ULEZ currently shares a boundary with the congestion zone but applies at all times. The daily charge of £12.50 (about US$16) applies to all emitting vehicles that enter central London and is in addition to the congestion charges. Ultra-low-emission vehicles are exempt: fully electric vehicles, plug-in hybrids, some regular hybrids, hydrogen-fuel-cell vehicles. Discounts are also available for taxis, residents, and persons with disabilities. These charges replace a series of pollution charges and discounts for greener vehicles that started as early as 2013. In 2021, the ULEZ is due to expand its coverage area to include much of Greater London.

I was in London the day of the launch. It was fascinating to see the media reporting on the concept. They had the predictable interviews with drivers who did not want to pay – but for the other side of the story, the BBC went to an elementary school in central London. It interviewed teachers, parents, and students. The air quality was so bad that the school had to supply asthma inhalers to students – the broadcast showed film of the rack used to store those inhalers. This angle to the story was not by accident – Mayor Kahn's team had done months of painstaking research and work into health and air-quality issues. The ULEZ was created as a solution to the real problem of air quality impacting the health of children and other residents, and they had ensured that the facts about the health impacts of poor air quality were well known. In this context, the launch of the zone was highly successful and the controversy limited, particularly compared to that surrounding Mayor Livingstone's original congestion charge.

London's buses are not exempt from LEZ and ULEZ charges. Although operated privately, buses are owned publicly. The city currently has a fleet of more than 200 electric buses in use in the ULEZ zone, along with more than 3,500 hybrid buses, 10 hydrogen-fuel-cell buses and new diesels that generate fewer emissions. Even the iconic double-decker buses are being replaced with hybrid, electric, or hydrogen versions. Starting in 2020, all new single-deck buses will be zero emissions, and by 2037 the entire bus fleet will be zero emission.

These measures are working. In 2017, London emitted enough pollution in the first five days of the year to breach its annual air pollution limits. In 2018, it took less than a month. But in 2019, when the ULEZ was fully operational, it took seven months. There is more to do, but the dramatic improvement in air quality shows the effectiveness of using regulatory authority and fees to encourage clean transportation choices. From the perspective of climate change, when air pollution from transportation is reduced, carbon pollution also drops because the pollution comes from the same source – the burning of fossil fuels.

Although controversial and politicized at commencement, the congestion charge and the subsequent ULEZ have proven to be popular and enduring. The congestion charge – aided by significant expansion of public transport – actually lowered congestion, and the ULEZ is cleaning the heavily polluted air. London's example shows clearly that as people experience the benefits of climate action firsthand and have an opportunity to adapt, they are supportive – and, in fact, they may be just as unwilling to lose the mobility and health benefits of these actions. Madrid is an interesting example of a political backlash against both congestion fees and their removal.

Madrid

Madrid, Spain – another centuries-old European capital with serious air quality and congestion issues – introduced an LEZ in its city center in 2018. High-emission vehicles were banned from the affected areas, with fines of up to €90 (about US$97) for noncompliance. Exemptions were provided for those who lived in the city center, but eventually all vehicles driving in the zone were to be required to be low-emission. In the meantime, the city was focusing on providing better public transportation and enabling walking and cycling.

The LEZ worked. Just six months after its implementation, air-pollution levels in the affected areas were at their lowest levels since 2010. Carbon-dioxide emissions were also significantly lower.

As in London, the LEZ in Madrid was controversial at inception. Certain drivers and car owners protested bitterly. Their complaints led to a movement to abolish the fees, and in the 2019 election José Luis Martínez-Almeida was elected as mayor on a platform that included abolishing the LEZ. On taking office he honored his promise. But what happened next was unexpected, certainly to the new mayor.

On June 29, 2019, during a scorching heat wave and just two days before the LEZ was to be dismantled, thousands of Madrid residents took to the streets. They used their voice to demand that the mayor reinstate the ban on polluting vehicles in the city center. "I want to breathe free" and "Defending the population from pollution" were some of the messages from the protesters. In addition, a petition calling for Madrid to keep its LEZ was signed by more than 220,000 people, a significant number out of the city's population of about six million. The message was clear: residents are willing to fight to preserve cleaner air and pedestrian-friendly streets.

As promised, and led by the new mayor, Madrid city center was opened to all vehicles on July 1, 2019. Air pollution in affected areas soared according to environmental groups. But the story did not end there. The residents also fought in the courts, and on July

5, 2019, a court ordered that the LEZ be reinstated. The judge specifically ruled that "the health of Madrid" trumps "the right to travel by car."

The fight in Madrid is revealing of the challenge of bold climate action. It is easy for politicians (typically but not always right wing) to fight actions that benefit health and our planet when the action threatens people's convenience. But people know that our health and climate-sustaining systems must take priority, and they will support strong and effective climate action. From a transportation perspective, we individually have choices in how we get around but we also have to take collective action to ensure that our air is fit to breathe and that our greenhouse gas emissions are sustainable.

On the Climate Front Lines

In many cities in Latin America and Asia there is a growing recognition that the transportation needs of a successful metropolis cannot be met by reliance on the private automobile, and these cities are taking steps to help provide individual transportation choices, particularly active transport (walking and cycling). Since 2013, Bengaluru, India, has made walking, cycling, and public transport a priority in its road-building tenders. As a result, ninety road projects (predominantly in the center of the city) have been reconstructed in ways that prioritize people rather than cars. The Colombian cities of Bogota and Bucaramanga have both undertaken projects to integrate and promote cycling as a safe, healthy alternative. Bucaramanga has a city cycling office and has been building the first of its reserved bike lanes; Bogota, under the leadership of then mayor Enrique Peñalosa, developed an integrated mobility plan (PIMS in Spanish) that has now resulted in 150,000 people actively commuting per day on safe cycling infrastructure built by the city – and enjoying themselves on Sunday mornings when more than one hundred kilometers (about sixty-two miles) of roads are closed to cars.

Making Active Transportation a Priority

Paris

In addition to ensuring that the vehicles entering a city center are cleaner, we can create more and better spaces for active transportation – that powered by people. Our feet, our bikes, and even our skateboards and scooters are better choices for our health and better for our climate. But in many cities the infrastructure has been built for the car – not for people. Still, there are examples of effective efforts to change this. Paris, for example, has been making a concerted effort to make active transportation an easy choice for its citizens.

Like London, Paris has a clear plan and has outlined the needed steps to become carbon neutral by 2050. The studies supporting its plan showed that in 2014, transportation accounted for 13 per cent of the city's emissions. Paris has recently ordered eight hundred electric buses and is making great progress in electrifying the parts of its public transportation system that use diesel and other fossil fuels. And again like London, Paris has LEZs, and restrictions are getting ever tighter: by 2030 only zero-emission vehicles will be allowed to drive in Paris. Unique to Paris, however, is its focus on walking and cycling – and the steps it is taking under the leadership of Mayor Anne Hidalgo to make active transportation easier and safer.

Every city has people who choose to walk and to bike. Making these activities easy and simple for most people allows them to choose walking and cycling as their routine way of going from place to place, but it requires rethinking how public spaces are used and challenging the dominance of the personal vehicle in transportation plans. This applies to any city, but the historic dominance of automobile-centered planning means that change takes political leadership and strong citizen participation. Paris has a unique combination of both.

Like most major cities, more than half of Paris's public space is currently devoted to the automobile, yet only 13 per cent of trips within the city take place in personal vehicles. These vehicles contribute disproportionally to air-quality issues in Paris.

In response to ideas raised by residents through Mayor Hidalgo's participatory budget and democracy initiatives, Paris has undertaken a redesign of its transportation infrastructure to put the needs of pedestrians and cyclists first. Introduced in 2017, the Pedestrian Paris Strategy (Paris Piéton) aims to create a network of connected pedestrian routes and to give over more of the road network to those on foot. The plan recognizes that pedestrians need to feel safe when walking and are more likely to choose to walk when they feel safe – particularly when their routes connect them to their destinations with attractive surroundings.

To increase both safety and the feeling of safety, intersections have been redesigned to give pedestrians more space, to improve visibility, to allow diagonal crossings, and to give pedestrians priority. Sidewalks, intersections, and other walking routes were reexamined with the goal of making them safer for those with mobility, visual, and other impairments. Measures were proposed to reduce traffic intensity. Seven major squares in Paris have been earmarked for redesign to reclaim space for human-powered mobility. And there are plans to replace the roads around the Eiffel Tower with gardens and pedestrian paths.

In some cases, separated spaces were developed for cyclists and for pedestrians to address safety concerns. Paris has also made a significant effort to improve the experience of walking – adding more benches and planters, creating meeting spaces at strategic locations, and adding more comfortable waiting spaces for transit stops. Artistic features and painted murals are being added to Paris's streets.

The city is also adding green spaces. Studies have shown that humans, especially children, benefit from interaction with nature. Even in urban settings, exposure to nature can lower stress, reduce anxiety, and ease depression. Neighborhoods in Paris have received support in transforming select roadways into green streets. Residents of these neighborhoods install and maintain planters, trees, and even replace strips of pavement with grass. In some areas, these streets are being shut down to vehicular traffic. It's a way to bring nature to a neighborhood while giving residents a reason to meet others in their community and discover how their own neighborhood can fill many of their basic needs.

Pockets of the city are regularly closed to vehicles. These areas are called Paris Respire (Paris Breathes) Zones. Depending on the area, it may be once a week, once a month, and throughout the year or only in the summer. Even the famous Champs Élysées is closed to traffic the first Sunday of each month. The goal is to have a Paris Respire Zone in every city area. Emergency vehicles and residents can still use the streets, but on the whole the streets belong to people on those special days, not to vehicles.

These days have been so successful that Paris has an annual citywide car-free day. City streets are shut down to all but essential motorized traffic. The people are invited to party, play games and sports, hold parades and races, go for bike rides, and enjoy being outdoors with fellow Parisians. This car-free day is enormously popular. And while residents learn how to live without a car for a day, they also enjoy a day with measurably lower air pollution and lower overall noise levels. Car-free days can demonstrate to people that it is possible to not use a car on other days, as well.

In addition, Paris has been investing in cycling infrastructure. A network of bike paths are being built with the goal of making all of Paris accessible by bike by the end of this year (2020), with more than seven hundred kilometers (435 miles) already built. At the launch of the plan, Mayor Hidalgo stated, "Our goal is to turn Paris into a global cycling capital."

To ensure all parts of the city are accessible and that cycling is safe, convenient, and pleasurable, Paris has developed a bike express network. Protected two-way continuous bike lanes were constructed on a north-south and east-west axis as well as on the banks of the Seine. Bike trails were added to two of the city's ring roads and two of its main boulevards.

A secondary network of bike lanes and trails extend from these main arteries. The speed limit for cars in all but the main roads of the city has been dropped to thirty kilometers (about eighteen miles) per hour to protect the safety of cyclists and encourage cycling. In fact, it has been suggested in the media that trip speeds in the city center are effectively faster by bike than by car.

Also included in the infrastructure plans are bike-parking spaces: ten thousand new spots are planned for strategic points around the city.

Building a pedestrian- and cycling-friendly city has not been without controversy, however. Pedestrianization of the Seine Quayside has been particularly contested. The roads running along the river Seine have acted as an urban highway through the city. The road on the Left Bank of the Seine Quayside was closed to vehicular traffic in 2013 and has since been popular with pedestrians and cyclists: in just three years, six million people took advantage of the space. But the Right Bank, pedestrianized in 2016, has been beset by lawsuits and controversy.

Paris City Council voted to close a 3.3 kilometer (two mile) stretch of the road on the Right Bank of the Seine Quayside in 2016. The area was to be redeveloped as gardens, cafés, and active-transportation paths. Extensive public consultations and stake-holder-engagement exercises were conducted, but not everyone felt heard. A commission of inquiry was launched due to complaints from those in the suburbs who were not part of the consultation. They felt that closure of the road would impact their commute times and that they should have been part of the process. The police force were concerned that the closure would increase response times. Motorists' and drivers' organizations claimed that the closure caused congestion and increased pollution levels: a common refrain for policies that challenge the transportation supremacy of the automobile.

In 2016, automobile advocates sued Paris in an effort to keep the Right Bank open to traffic. The city lost the case as the court found procedural problems with the impact assessments related to vehicle traffic, road pollution, and noise levels; however, the city won on appeal. Today, the roadway remains closed to traffic, and plans are in progress to replace the pavement along the road with grass. The pedestrianization was a difficult political fight, but one that appears to have ended successfully with Mayor Hidalgo's overwhelming reelection in June 2020.

A bank of Vélib' bicycles, ready for Parisians and tourists outside of station rue Lepic, Montmartre. Paris's successful bikeshare program sparked worldwide interest and similar initiatives. Source: Paul Gueu/iStockphoto.com.

All these steps have been significant and effective – in Paris, carbon emissions from transport are down markedly, as are emissions from fine particulate matter. London emissions are reduced as well, and air quality is much improved. These are important steps toward a low-carbon city – and as shown by London, addressing the type of vehicles driving in the city matters greatly as well.

On the Climate Front Lines

Bike sharing – short-term rentals of bicycles – has become a very popular method of urban transportation and is a good example of how effective city ideas can spread. The first such system was started in Paris – the Vélib' Metropole. Launched in 2007, it now has more than 23,000 bikes and over 1,300 docking stations. In one month alone (August 2019) more than 8.5 million kilometers were covered by trips on Vélib'. After Paris introduced the program, representatives from numerous cities came to Paris to learn about the bikeshare system. The result has been an explosion in the number of bikeshare programs globally: estimates put the number at more than one thousand in 2016. By trying new approaches, sharing lessons learned, and responding to the demands of riders, bikeshare programs are getting better and better.

Making Electric Vehicles Possible: EV Charging

By 2050, London will allow only zero-emission vehicles within the city. With the intended expansion and tightening of the ULEZ, it is becoming increasingly expensive and ultimately will become impossible to drive internal combustion engines in London. By 2030, the only new vehicles registered to drive in London will be zero emission. To make this possible, an expansive electric vehicle (EV) charging network is required, as a lack of charging infrastructure is a significant barrier to EV adoption in cities.

London first started developing a public charging network in 2011. By the end of 2020, the city will have installed 300 rapid chargers and 3,500 regular chargers. By 2025, the numbers are expected to be approximately 3,000 rapid and nearly 50,000 regular chargers. The city is well on its way to achieving its goals.

Installing chargers sounds straightforward, but technical challenges make large-scale implementation complex. For example, at the moment, a single standardized charging port does not exist.

There are also concerns about how EV charging will affect the electricity grid. As transportation becomes electrified, the demand for electricity increases. Upgrades to the power grid will be necessary, capacity may need to be increased, and engineers will need to find ways to be smarter about how EVs use electricity – for example, can the batteries be used to store energy to support the grid, particularly to support intermittent sources of electricity such as wind?

In the future, utilities may be able to allow an EV battery to recharge when overall power demand is low and take power from the EV battery when demand spikes. A car that's plugged in while the owner is asleep or at the office can therefore help to manage the gaps the utility sees between supply and demand of electricity. A good idea, but one that requires considerable planning for an electricity-distribution network that can utilize distributed energy storage.

Those are not the only challenges. Cities are densely developed, and finding convenient places to add charging infrastructure can be challenging. Car owners must have confidence that there'll be enough chargers in accessible locations before they'll be willing to choose an electric vehicle (a problem referred to as "range anxiety").

This complexity means that adding EV charging stations to a city involves input from many different institutions. For the City of London, developing a network of EV-charging infrastructure involves 35 different planning authorities and consultations with more than 140 organizations and more than 350 stakeholders. Getting this number of organizations to work together to find solutions is a huge challenge – but at its best, it's a great source of ideas, innovations, and opportunities for collaboration.

Transportation for London ("TfL," the municipal organization responsible for transportation) oversees the city's efforts to install chargers. To build the system, TfL has been collaborating with the private sector and supporting shared business charging infrastructure.

The plans are working. In 2018, plug-in vehicles represented 2.8 per cent of new car registrations in London. The city has installed 178 rapid chargers, 72 of these devoted exclusively to taxis. The private sector has added another 24. By the summer of 2019, 2,250 slow to fast chargers were operational. The city's target of 300 rapid chargers and 3,500 slow to fast chargers by the end of 2020 seems entirely achievable. A call center has also been established to provide around-the-clock customer support.

London shows us what is possible. Its congestion charge and ULEZ have manifestly improved transportation, air quality, and people's lives. These successes have made it possible for the city to be aggressive on policies regarding electric vehicles – people want to live in a city with clean air, where it is easier and safer to get around. These programs build a political constituency for action, demonstrating a way forward for other cities that do not know where to start.

This kind of city leadership matters. A significant transition to clean, non-polluting vehicles needs to happen rapidly if we are to keep the world on a 1.5 degree path. Another important strategy for cities is to address the owners of huge vehicle fleets – starting with themselves,

City Fleets Go Zero Emission

Cities themselves own significant fleets. From cars to heavy construction machinery, garbage trucks to police cars, parks vehicles to fire trucks, cities are significant owners and operators of vehicles. Centralized ownership of fleets is an advantage when considering environmental impact – vehicles can be "right sized." (For instance, does a parks supervisor need to drive a pickup truck or will a hybrid do? Does a parking-ticket officer need a minivan or can they walk, cycle, and use transit?) It is easier to install and operate EV charging stations for fleets, particularly for those with set, regular operating hours. And, as will be discussed later, cities have regulatory authority or influence over some other fleets – and where they do not, they have a bully pulpit to demand change.

Significant strides are being made to dramatically reduce reliance on gasoline or diesel-powered fleets. It is now possible to order electric garbage and recycling trucks, cars, police interceptors, pickup trucks, and most other vehicles in a city fleet. It is also possible to buy hybrid vehicles for almost everything else, and these purchases are cost effective because these vehicles are heavily used, and therefore provide savings on fuel and maintenance over their gasoline- and diesel-powered counterparts. New York City, a leader in the greening of fleets, has gone from 211 electric vehicles in 2014 to more than 2,200 today, with plans to have 4,000 by 2025. When added to hybrids and right sizing, the city estimates that it has saved nine thousand metric tons of CO_2 and an average of US$550 per year per vehicle in maintenance costs.

Private Fleets

Cities have control over their own fleets but also have significant power over private-sector fleets – sometimes by contract (for example, when garbage and recycling are collected by a private-sector hauler), and sometimes by regulation. Cities regulate taxis. They have the authority to regulate electronically dispatched vehicles for hire (such as Lyft vehicles), and they often license other fleets or have some regulatory authority over them, such as business licenses.

City Action Works: Taxis

Progress does not need to be slow. In Oslo, Norway, zero-emission vehicle adoption (primarily through electric vehicles) is significant.

Norway has created powerful incentives for EV adoption by taxing the purchase of gasoline and diesel cars at high rates and also subsidizing EV purchase. Oslo, its capital, has a congestion charge and bus lanes, both of which give preference to EVs. These measures together have resulted in interesting examples of EV adoption, including in business fleets. For example, Oslo is partnering with the local electricity utility and an American developer of wireless EV charging infrastructure to develop a wireless system for charging taxis. The chargers will be placed at taxi stands, allowing the cars to be recharged while waiting for their next fare. Through this technology, the city is planning an all zero-emission taxi fleet by 2023.

Oslo is not alone. Shenzhen, China, the world leader in EVs, has a fleet of taxis that is almost entirely electric – reducing emissions by nearly one million tons of CO_2 per year. There are nearly twenty-two thousand taxis in Shenzhen, and the city has been innovative in moving to EVs. Thousands of chargers have been installed to support these taxis, and these chargers may also be used by personal EVs. Some of the chargers are embedded in streetlight poles: a clever solution as these are often located near street parking and already have access to the electrical grid. This modification also facilitates the more widespread and easy use of EVs by the general public, as access to charging helps to address range anxiety.

London, England, has adopted policies supporting the electrification of taxis. Many current taxis are hybrid, and the iconic London black cab is now available as an all-electric model, launched to satisfy the city's regulatory requirements. (The company that manufactures these cabs recently announced a hiring increase at its UK plant to meet the increased demand for electric taxis in London and in other cities that are following London's lead.)

Since 2018, new taxi licenses are given only to vehicles that are zero-emission capable, including full electric, hydrogen, and some hybrid vehicles. The age limit for existing taxis will be reduced from fifteen to twelve years by 2022, and a fund is available to help convert internal combustion engine taxis to cleaner liquid petroleum gas. To further support electric taxis, the city's installation of rapid charging points particularly considers locations for taxi use. These standards are being applied in a modified form to electronically dispatched vehicles for hire and other personal-hire vehicles as well.

Private Delivery Fleets – Untapped Potential

The transformation of city-owned fleets can lead to a market transformation, through demonstrating that EVs (and other zero-emission vehicles) can be used successfully in a large busy fleet. Cities assist by providing a market for vehicle manufacturers, and city policies can encourage the move to clean transportation.

But in some places, the private sector has been very slow to adapt; for example, the fleets operated by post offices and couriers. These fleets typically (but not exclusively) use popular models of vans. The fleets are significant – Federal Express estimates its fleet at eighty-five thousand vehicles, the US post office nearly two hundred thousand, and Canada Post seven thousand. While some efforts have been made to acquire more fuel-efficient vehicles, very few of these fleet owners have made a public commitment to electrify or otherwise create zero-emission fleets. Yet many of the popular models of vans they use have electric versions that have been available for years; today there are models by Mercedes, Nissan, Renault, and other major manufacturers that average more than 150 kilometers (about 93 miles) per day and are well suited for delivery fleets with central distribution hubs where they can be charged. There are smaller manufacturers as well, and DHL has a partnership with Ford to manufacture the ubiquitous Ford Transit in an electric version. Amazon has announced that it will buy one hundred thousand EVs by 2030 (through its ownership of a vehicle-manufacturer startup named Rivian). Some companies are exploring fuel cells and other zero- or low-emission technologies. This is all good news – but a sense of urgency is lacking. We're in a climate emergency, yet most of these companies and government agencies have done little to transform their fleets at the scale and pace required over the past decade.

These fleets are largely regulated nationally or at the subnational (state or province) level, where despite the rhetoric of some elected officials, there seems to be no action commensurate with the scale of the climate challenge. Concerns include cost of acquisition and need to build infrastructure. However, EVs are vastly less expensive to run and maintain, making the cost of ownership reasonable. Without strong policy direction from governments, progress will be slow – except in cities such as London, where the added cost of running polluting vehicles in the ULEZ is already motivating a transition to clean fleets. It is expected that more and more city governments will find ways to encourage this transition, given the huge number of delivery vehicles operating on their streets every day.

The Final Word

Greenhouse gas emissions in major cities include significant emissions from cars and trucks, particularly in spread-out cities built to favor private cars over public transport. A significant portion of these emissions – as much as 25 per cent – can be addressed through policies that make cities easier places to walk, ride, and use an EV (or a zero-emission alternative). Policies in place today show that cities can both regulate transport and provide access to infrastructure (such as charging points) that can help rapidly accelerate the use of electric cars, taxis, and other fleets. This transformation can make it easier for people to opt for low-pollution choices and drive market change (and increase employment). Because these changes make cities cleaner, healthier, and better places to live, they have proved to be popular and enduring, even though initially controversial.

Chapter 7

Waste

The statistics on the amount of waste we produce are truly mind-boggling. The electronic revolution alone has produced incredible quantities of waste – according to The World Counts, forty million tons of e-waste per year, The equivalent of throwing away eight hundred laptops per second. And that's just the beginning. We throw away 4.5 trillion cigarette butts, 25 billion Styrofoam coffee cups – in the US alone. What's more, 480 billion plastic bottles of water are sold each year, and "fast fashion" – clothes designed to be worn only a few times and then discarded – has developed as a trend the past few years. Then there are plastic bags. Straws. And much, much more. We live in a society that produces staggering amounts of waste, all of which has to be disposed of somewhere.

***

It wasn't always this way.

In the English village where I grew up in the 1960s, almost nothing was thrown away, because in the post-war economy people had very little money and so were careful to fix what was broken. If they could not fix it, a local service (the rag-and-bone man) would buy it and fix it for resale. Products were built to last – the classic example is the telephone. When telephone companies were owned by the government, or were privately owned but publicly regulated, they typically owned the telephones and leased them to their customers. In this context, it made economic sense to build telephones to last – according to one article, for up to twenty-five years. Today, across the entire range of things people buy, it is very different. Whether this is caused by built-in obsolescence (deliberately making products not to last so that we have to buy new ones relatively quickly) or a change in attitudes can be debated, but the result is clear – ever-increasing mountains of waste. Just look at the iPhone: in the thirteen years since it was introduced, there have been eleven models. And all of the used phones need to be disposed. The waste keeps piling up.

Cities Manage the Disposal of Waste

New York City produces more than fourteen million tons of waste each year, Toronto nearly a million from residential sources only – and Accra, Ghana, more than five hundred thousand tons. In Accra and many cities in the developing world, waste management is a critical public health and safety issue, as overflowing waste from informal waste disposal often blocks storm sewers. After a bad storm, nearby beaches are covered in trash – plastic bags, bottles, and other litter. There are huge blobs of plastic in the ocean, growing larger and larger. These blobs are becoming dead zones in the middle of the ocean. Located halfway between Hawaii and California, the Great Pacific Garbage Patch spans 1.6 million square kilometers, an area twice the size of Texas. An estimated 1.6 trillion pieces of plastic float in the patch – equivalent to 250 pieces for every person

The impact of this waste on wildlife is shocking. Fish frequently are found to have ingested significant amounts of microscopic (and toxic) plastic; seabirds are found with plastic straws stuck in their throats; and whales, turtles, dolphins, and other sea creatures become ensnared in fishing nets. Source: Yamtono_Sardi/iStockphoto.com.

in the world. Because it does not biodegrade, the plastic simply gets smaller and smaller – eventually becoming potential feed for fish and other sea creatures, ultimately creating health hazards for people. Like these giant blobs in the ocean, the amount of garbage we produce seems uncontrollable.

Proliferating waste from a society with ever-higher demands for disposable items is a huge problem for nature. It is also a problem for cities, because almost every city in the world is responsible for the administration of its waste. Our economic system treats more and more things as disposable, and that creates massive challenges for cities – including waste's impact on climate. If waste isn't disposed of carefully, it can be a significant source of methane gas. Rotting food combined with other materials produces methane, and in a traditional waste system where all "trash" is collected and sent to landfills, the methane escapes to the atmosphere. The best modern systems separate the compostable waste, then capture and treat the methane.

Methane: A Powerful Problem

Methane is a potent greenhouse gas. It is far more powerful in trapping heat in the atmosphere than carbon dioxide (twenty to ninety times more powerful, depending on the timeframe). Methane degrades to CO_2 over time – about twelve years – and remains in the atmosphere, contributing to long-term warming of the earth's atmosphere. Although less than 20 per cent of global greenhouse gas emissions came from methane in 2017, the fact that those emissions are so powerful means that actions to address them are significant. As with CO_2 emissions, methane emissions have been dramatically increasing (see Figure 7.1).

Much of that methane comes from agricultural sources: livestock, rice cultivation, synthetic fertilizers, manures. And the energy sector is responsible for methane emissions from coal mining and natural-gas systems.

In cities, most methane emissions come from waste: organic food and yard waste, and from wastewater treatment. As food and yard waste break down in the absence of oxygen, much of their carbon is converted to methane.

According to Project Drawdown (a project founded in 2014 by environmentalist Paul Hawken to research solutions to climate change), over the course of a century, methane has thirty-four times the greenhouse effect of carbon dioxide. Landfills are a top source of methane emissions, releasing 12 per cent of the world's total. Landfill methane can be tapped, captured, and used as a fairly clean energy source for generating electricity or heat, rather than leaking into the air or being dispersed as waste. The climate benefit from this is twofold: it prevents landfill emissions and displaces the coal, oil, or natural gas that might otherwise be used.

Cities have three main options to reduce methane emissions from waste: capturing the methane at a traditional landfill or collecting organic matter separately and using aerobic or anaerobic digestion facilities to compost the waste that will either use the methane as a fuel (thereby significantly reducing its climate impact) or turn the methane into carbon dioxide.

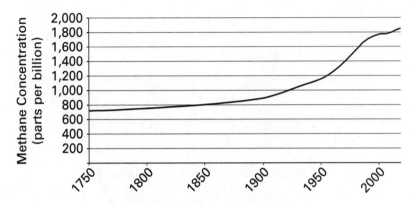

Figure 7.1: Global Atmospheric Concentration of Methane, 1750 – 2018
Source: Based on data from the European Environmental Agency (EEA) and the National Oceanic and Atmospheric Administration (NOAA).

Incineration of waste is not considered a viable option by climate advocates and scientists. When garbage is burned, toxic substances such as heavy metals may be released into the environment. Furthermore, plastics and other materials in the waste generate carbon dioxide. Since plastics are generally made from fossil fuels, incineration has an impact similar to burning fossil fuels.

Cities Committed to Zero Waste

In addition to emissions from waste disposal, our cycle of consumption leads to emissions throughout the creation and consumption of goods. Some cities are aiming for a zero-waste system. It isn't just a question of managing our resources sustainably: it is also a question of reducing the climate impact of our waste. It takes energy to extract resources, process them into usable goods, and transport them to their destinations. When we rethink how we consume, reduce the goods we waste, reuse goods, and recycle materials, we are also reducing the associated emissions (see Figure 7.2). Take aluminum: recycling an aluminum can into a new one takes as little as 5 per cent of the energy it takes to make a can from virgin material (i.e., bauxite), and that

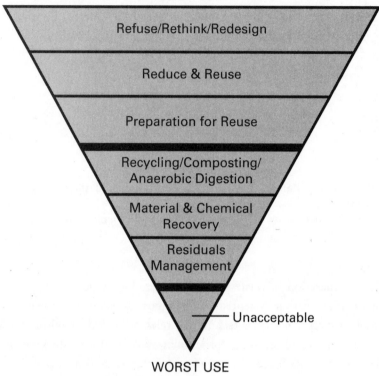

Figure 7.2: Hierarchy of Action
This chart shows clearly the environmental hierarchy of action – recycling is important, but redesigning and reducing are far more important. Source: Adapted from Zero Waste Europe, A Zero Waste Hierarchy, www .zerowasteeurope.eu/2019/05/a-zero-waste-hierarchy-for-europe/.

energy might come from burning fossil fuels. Cities committing to zero waste are therefore undertaking an important climate strategy.

San Francisco Takes the Lead

San Francisco is a city with steep hills, a vibrant waterfront, and a strong and growing economy. Like other cities mentioned in this book, San Francisco has a clear plan to have net-zero emissions by 2050. It has already made impressive gains. The city's first climate-action plan was released in 2004 under the leadership of then mayor Gavin Newsom (although work began under the previous mayor, Willie Brown). At that time, it was one of the first community climate-action plans in the United States. By 2017, San Francisco had surpassed its original goals: emission reductions had exceeded the intermediate target, at 36 per cent below 1990 levels. This was despite a large increase in population and a huge increase in GDP. (San Francisco has clearly demonstrated that carbon emissions can be dissociated from GDP and population growth.) As part of this work, San Francisco has become a world leader in waste management.

Waste represented 6 per cent of the city's total emissions in 2017, and the goal is to reduce that number to zero – meaning 100 per cent diversion of discarded materials to recycling and composting. Recent changes to global recycling systems may extend the time it takes to reach that goal, but San Francisco's strategy has been so successful that it is being widely adopted elsewhere.

There were multiple motivations for the zero-waste program: to conserve resources, to reduce waste's environmental impact, to create jobs, to save money (waste disposal is a significant drain on a city's resources), and to reduce greenhouse gas emissions. San Francisco also made the case that going to zero waste would improve the air quality from energy conservation and reduced manufacturing, and that their approach to waste could potentially mean the creation of community waste/recycling facilities and the associated employment.

San Francisco has an unusual history for waste collection and processing. In 1932, a refuse ordinance was passed that created permit areas where waste collection companies could get exclusive rights for waste collection. The bylaw gave the city authority to set the rates for waste collection. Over time, one company, now named Recology, bought all the permits in the city and became the city's sole waste collector.

Recology is 100 per cent employee owned and cooperates with the city in its ambitious goals for waste management. It collects and processes all of San Francisco's waste, and is an interesting example of a business working with a city to accomplish important public policy goals. (Note: Concerns about Recology's monopoly led to a citywide referendum in 2012 on a proposition to separate waste collection into multiple competitive bid contracts. The proposition was defeated, and Recology continues to be San Francisco's sole operator for solid waste collection and processing.)

San Francisco and Recology are taking a simple approach in working toward zero waste, one that is considered state of the art by most progressive city governments. In order of priority, the first goal is waste prevention, then reducing and reusing waste. What remains is targeted for recycling and composting.

To prevent waste generation, the city has instituted several bans on packaging. Over time, some forms of plastic bags, takeout containers, water bottles, and other single-use packaging have been banned.

In 2007, large grocery stores and retailers were prohibited from using single-use plastic bags. Only certified compostable plastic bags or paper bags with post-consumer content were allowed as checkout bags, and these had to be sold, not given away. Reusable bags were also encouraged, but to qualify for use by a retailer, these had to be washable and able to withstand more than 125 uses. By 2013, this ordinance applied to all retail stores and food establishments. It is estimated that San Francisco has reduced its disposable checkout-bag usage by 70 to 90 per cent as a consequence of this city law. Plastic bags are a common source of litter, a common contaminant in recycling and composting systems, and take time to break down in landfills. More than seventy-five other cities and counties in California have followed San Francisco's lead in banning plastic bags.

The city has also led efforts to hold producers of waste responsible for it – rather than the purchasers of their product. In 2006, it passed the Extended Producer Responsibility Resolution to lobby for state legislation to increase producer responsibility for a product's full lifecycle. The city believes in creating incentives for product redesign to minimize waste, as well as measures to make producers and distributors responsible for product recycling and disposal. San

Francisco's efforts particularly target producers of hazardous waste. The net effect is to shift the cost of recycling and disposal away from municipalities toward the producers and distributors of the materials – giving them an economic incentive to avoid creating the waste in the first place.

One successful example of extended producer responsibility is the 2015 Safe Drug Disposal Stewardship Ordinance. With this city law, drug manufacturers are required to provide San Francisco residents with a safe and convenient way to dispose of their unwanted prescription and over-the-counter medication. The goal was to prevent pharmaceutical products from polluting aquatic ecosystems, to help combat prescription drug abuse, and to address a category of products that are not served by conventional waste collection. More than forty-four medicine-collection kiosks are located throughout the city where residents can drop off unwanted medications. Alternatively, prepaid mail-back envelopes are available. In 2018, a total of 23,474 pounds (10,648 kilograms) of medicines were collected as a result of this ordinance.

In 2009, San Francisco introduced a mandatory recycling and composting program that built on the food-waste composting program that's been operational since the 1990s. Residents are required to separate their waste into three bins: recycling (blue bin), compostable waste (green bin), and trash (black bin). Note that unlike programs in many other cities, separating waste is a *requirement*. When waste is incorrectly sorted, educational material is provided to residents in a variety of languages. However, repeat offenders can be fined.

To encourage greater separation of waste, the size of the black trash bin is shrinking, while the size of the recycling and compost bins remains large. Residents who are unable to fit their trash into the smaller black bins must pay extra to use a larger one, and they may be subject to a waste audit. Waste audits are also performed regularly at sites that consistently generate large volumes of waste. (In some cities, this can be controversial, particularly at inception, but in San Francisco, Toronto, and elsewhere the practice has become widely accepted.) The compost program is highly successful and effective in reducing methane emissions and therefore minimizing the impact on climate change. Compost is used to fertilize California vineyards, and the city has facilities that use anaerobic digestion of compostable products to generate biogas for collection fleets and buildings.

Apartment buildings remain a significant challenge in San Francisco, as in all cities. More than half of San Francisco's residents live in apartment buildings, the majority of which are outfitted with only one garbage chute (except for newer buildings, which have multiple waste chutes for separated collection). Typically, in the older buildings, trash is deposited in the chute, but recyclables and compost must be carried down to basement-storage areas, a disincentive to recycling and composting. As it is very expensive to retrofit buildings to have a multi-chute system, this practice tends to be the norm.

On the Climate Front Lines

The challenge of separating waste in multi-residential buildings is faced by other cities as well, as until very recently buildings were universally designed with one garbage chute, based on the principle that everything could just be thrown away. In Toronto, one building in Scarborough (Mayfair on the Green) has addressed this challenge by reversing the process – compost is deposited down the garbage chute, and garbage and recycling taken downstairs by hand. This change took considerable leadership by the superintendent, Princely Soundranayagam, and an ability to work patiently with building residents to help them understand the changes. Happily, economic interests – garbage pickup is expensive, but compost and recycling are free – and a desire to do the right thing persuaded the residents that Princely's ideas were correct. The building now stands as a wonderful example of what is possible with strong leadership and even stronger listening.

To address this challenge, San Francisco plans to improve the extraction of recyclables and compost from the collected waste stream from multi-residential buildings, develop the market for recyclables and compost, and introduce more material bans.

The city also provides oversight and carries out research and outreach activities. City departments must have well-designed recycling, composting, and trash areas, and events organized or authorized by the city require event organizers to attend zero-waste training and offer recycling and composting. The city has banned the sale and distribution of plastic water bottles on city property and has increased the availability of drinking water in public spaces.

San Francisco is advanced in dealing with construction waste. Current rules require a minimum of 65 per cent of construction, demolition, and remodeling waste material to be diverted from landfill, and large new commercial and residential buildings must divert a minimum of 75 per cent of construction waste and meet LEED Materials and Resources credit 2 requirements (targets for recovering, reusing, recycling materials). This is part of a significant series of measures, some internal – demonstrating leadership and what's possible – and some external.

Internally, the city has an active plan to address the reduction of waste and the purchase of more sustainable products. The approved product list emphasizes recycled content – for example, 100 per cent post-consumer-content recycled paper. City departments must appoint a recycling coordinator, assess their waste, submit a resource-conservation plan, submit an annual recycling survey, and report on solid-waste diversion. They are required to reuse office furniture, computers, and supplies using a virtual-warehouse exchange system, and even print two-sided on paper.

The city has taken the lessons it's learned and worked to assist residents and businesses. It created an online database of local businesses that divert 75 per cent or more of their waste; it offers waste audits and consultations to businesses; has programs for pickup of specialized, toxic, or large waste items (such as scrap metal, electronics, motor oil, batteries, fluorescent bulbs); and has a team ("the Environment Now" team) that conducts extensive outreach and education for residents and businesses, and checks curbside bins for compliance.

The city is planning to add a zero-waste facility to improve processing efficiencies and recover compostable and recyclable goods that have not been source separated. To assist in moving toward zero waste, the city is considering the introduction of more material bans and waste-prevention campaigns, and continues to encourage producer-responsibility initiatives, some of which are also being considered by the State Government of California.

On the Climate Front Lines

Sao Paolo is a large, sprawling industrial city of some twelve million people. It faces many of the challenges of large cities in South America – poverty, transportation issues, and a lack of basic infrastructure in the barrios outside the city. Yet Sao Paulo is a leader in addressing methane emissions from landfill – an important goal of its climate-action plan. In both 2007 and 2009 it closed landfills and installed systems to capture the landfill gas and use it to generate electricity. These systems generate a meaningful part of Sao Paulo's electricity – about 7 per cent (175,000 megawatt hours). Sao Paulo's financing of the project was also innovative: it applied and qualified for funding from the UN Clean Development mechanism. It was also awarded carbon credits (shared with the biogas company) and earned more than €26 million in credits.

Waste Transformation in Global Cities

Ljubljana

The ideas used in San Francisco can work almost everywhere. Ljubljana, Slovenia, is an excellent case study of what can be done, moving rapidly from recently starting separated waste collection to building a foundation for an economy that effectively reuses products rather than throwing them out – an idea known as a circular economy.

Ljubljana is the capital of Slovenia and has overseen a transformational change in the way it deals with waste. Separated waste collection began only in 2002, but by 2014, the city was diverting more than 60 per cent of its waste to recycling and composting facilities. Even its total per capita waste generation is impressive: the annual per person output of waste in 2014 was a mere 167 kilograms (368 pounds), while the European average was 475 kilograms (1,047 pounds) and the US average an astonishing 743 kilograms (1,638 pounds). Waste reduction and diversion was so effective that in 2014 the city scrapped its plans to build the country's first waste-incineration plant.

Ljubljana has worked closely with the public waste-management company Snaga to develop strategies to achieve zero waste. Once curbside pickup of separated recycling and compost was established in 2013, Snaga began to reduce the frequency of garbage pickup. Across the city, recycling and compost is picked up two to three times more frequently than garbage. This initially led to complaints, opposition, and packed garbage containers. Through education campaigns on sorting, open discussions of the reasons for the changes, and videos showing how those packed garbage containers were full of recyclable and compostable substances, the public mood eased, and the changes were accepted.

In Ljubljana, hazardous waste, large items, metals, textiles, e-waste, and other materials are collected in collection centers scattered across the city. Recognizing that these centers may not be convenient or accessible to all residents, mobile collection units are sent out to the neighborhoods twice a year to pick up these items. Free pickup of bulky items can be arranged. A recent measure in densely populated centers is pay-per-use pricing for disposal of garbage and compostable materials. Access to recycling bins remains free.

The city's focus has now shifted to waste reduction and the building of a circular economy. By promoting leasing instead of buying, services instead of products, and sharing instead of ownership, the city saw an opportunity to reduce waste and build a more livable city. A "Get Used to Reusing" campaign was launched and later adopted nationally. This was supported with the establishment of a reuse center, a clothing e-library, bike-sharing and electric car-sharing services, a library of things (for borrowing tools, sports equipment, etc.), exchange depots, a Repair Cafe, and a public company that makes paper towels and toilet paper from milk and juice packaging. Snaga, the waste-management company, even furnished its offices with upcycled and reused furniture. At the industrial level, they encourage symbiosis: where waste from one industry is used as raw material for another local company. Ljubljana is showing the world how a shift in thinking can lead to the elimination of nearly all waste.

As a result of these efforts, the city won the European Commission's Green Capital Award in 2016 for waste management. The city is building on this success by focusing on ambitious goals: reducing the amount of residual waste to 60 kilograms (132 pounds) per person annually by 2025, and to 50 kilograms (110 pounds) by 2035. It plans to increase the diversion rate to 78 per cent by 2025 and 80 per cent by 2035, with an ultimate goal of zero waste – the first European capital to aim for zero waste.

Ljubljana makes an interesting study for a North American audience: we often seem to assume that we have all the answers and, implicitly, that other parts of the world – developing nations, Eastern Europe, Africa – must learn from us. As shown in this case, the learning is often a two-way process. Another case is Accra, Ghana, where the city has addressed multiple public policy goals by addressing waste management.

Accra

Accra is a large sprawling city with multiple challenges. As is often the case in Africa, large informal settlements lack basic services, and the residents lack decent work. The lack of basic services can lead to problems not just with the service gap, but also in public health and welfare in general.

Prior to 2016, waste management as a basic service did not exist in Accra's informal settlements. As a result, garbage was left in informal (and illegal) garbage dumps, where it was burned in the open, creating air pollution and fire hazards in addition to public health challenges. Garbage was collected from residents by an informal system of waste pickers – individuals who, for a small fee, collected garbage and left it at the dumps, making very little money in the process. (More than three hundred tons of garbage was collected daily by the waste pickers, and, including other sources, more than six hundred tons made its way to the dumps.)

In 2016, Accra, under the leadership of Mayor Mohammed Adjei Sowah, began the process of closing these illegal dumps. The closures happened in 2017, and the dumps were replaced by three regular transfer stations. To maintain social equity, the city ensured that the informal waste pickers could still find work – recognizing them as legitimate and increasing opportunities for them to earn income (for example, from recycling and selling reusable products). More than six hundred such workers have been registered with the city, which has helped to dignify their work, stabilize their employment, and increase their incomes.

Stable employment has also helped increase collection and recycling rates in Accra. The initiative's impact on climate is important too. The city's carbon footprint has shrunk as waste is no longer burned, and methane no longer seeps from the informal landfills. In addition, the positioning of transfer stations in more central locations means fewer vehicle miles are being driven for waste-related matters. Some estimates by the city show significant greenhouse gas reductions from these efforts – and public health benefits too. Accra has not had an outbreak of cholera since 2017.

While informal waste collection and illegal dumping at this scale is not a problem in most cities in the developed world, addressing climate change in a way that is equitable and supports workers' transition to more sustainable practices is a challenge that all cities face. Accra demonstrates that it is eminently feasible to have a just transition for workers while achieving critical environmental goals.

"The future we want recognizes the crucial role of the informal sector in sustainable city development. Combating climate change requires inclusive decision making which ensures all citizens are a part of the solution, to be acting local to impact positively on global challenges."

– Mohammed Adjei Sowah (Accra), 2019

The Final Word

In virtually every country in the world, cities are responsible for managing waste. We face a huge collective challenge with the ever-increasing amount of things made with the expectation they will simply be thrown away. This increasing mountain of garbage poses a challenge for our environment on several fronts – including greenhouse gas emissions. Effective waste management – particularly separating compostable waste and capturing landfill gas – can lower a city's greenhouse gas emissions by 5 to 6 per cent – possibly more in cities in the developing world with large informal settlements and informal dumps. The methods to do so are proven and adaptable to all cities globally. As part of a broader waste-management plan, a city can lower greenhouse gas emissions, stop pollution, and address economic challenges as well – all by using these proven and time-tested ideas. Even more can be done by finding ways to create a circular economy, ensuring that the waste is not produced to begin with – or that it can be repurposed for other uses rather than simply thrown out.

Epilogue

The title of this book – *Solved* – is provocative. Deliberately so. But is it true to say that the climate crisis can be solved in cities? Yes. Entirely by cities? Perhaps not, although it is in cities that we can do the most important thing to address the climate crisis: act now. The contributions by cities to lowering emissions from electricity generation, transportation, buildings, and waste are real. If the best existing strategies are replicated quickly at scale, they can make the material difference needed now by dramatically lowering the emissions that cause climate change. Published reports have concluded city action can reduce greenhouse gas emissions by as much as two-thirds, possibly even by 70 to 75 per cent. Most important, cities can solve the climate crisis because they're doing what is most urgently needed today – taking effective action at scale to get dramatic results over the next decade.

Studies show that in the developed world, emissions need to peak very soon and start dropping – halving by 2030, on the way to net zero by 2050 – if we are to have any hope of avoiding the worst of climate change. For large cities – certainly the members of the C40 – the requirement of science is that the emissions from those urban areas must peak no later than the end of 2020, and be on a path to be (collectively) halved by 2030. The good news is that by the end of 2019, thirty-four of those cities had already peaked emissions, and more than one hundred (C40 and non-C40) had committed to having a plan to do exactly that. And the further good news is that, using the projects and programs mentioned in this book, along with others, it is possible to get the world on track by 2030.

I first truly realized the global effectiveness of city-based action at the UN Climate Change Conference (COP15) in Copenhagen, Denmark, in November 2009. I knew, of course, that cities were leaders – I had seen action by mayors on global issues like SARS, the 2008 financial crisis, and climate change. But being in Copenhagen brought home the fact that it was really only cities that were taking major action to address climate change on the international stage. It also demonstrated to me that people were with the mayors – that they expected and demanded leadership on climate change, regardless of what a few loud voices said in opposition.

COP15, in Denmark, was supposed to be the moment in which the nations of the world came to agreement about measures to address the climate crisis. It was in a country that was a leader, significant diplomatic work had already been done, and the United States had a new and dynamic president who wanted the world to address climate change. There was a recipe for success. But the negotiations failed.

At the same time that the negotiations were in the midst of collapsing, at a convention center outside the main city, near the airport, the mayors of more than one hundred cities attended the Copenhagen Climate Summit for Mayors, right in the center of town – in the square beside city hall. The mayors were united in showing their actions – united behind the slogan "While Nations Talk, Cities Act." The then mayor of Copenhagen, Ritt Bjerregaard, and I cohosted the event – mayors from every continent attended. Work done by these cities to reduce greenhouse gases was on display every day. It generated buzz and excitement – so much so that cities were the cover story on the newspaper being printed for the delegates to the COP. The contrast could not have been more stark. More than one hundred mayors, effectively using the powers and influence they had in public transit, buildings, active transportation, development, waste management, traffic reduction, energy, and much more to reduce emissions. They were effective, creative, and passionate – Mayor Bjerregaard had even commissioned MIT to invent a new electric-powered bicycle for the occasion – and the contrast with national governments (lacking urgency, ineffective, and disorganized) could not have been more clear. It was abundantly clear to me at that moment that if the world had hope to address climate change, that hope had to start with the leadership and actions of cities.

Today, thousands of cities are acting to address climate change and have made long-term commitments. It's hard to know precisely how many cities are on track to meet what science requires, because their actions and commitments are not always captured and measured externally.

The leading network of major cities – C40 Cities – does commit its members to both science-based targets and external monitoring of achievements. As I write this book, the chair, Mayor Eric Garcetti of Los Angeles, and the elected steering committee of mayors are engaging hundreds of other mayors of major cities to agree to those commitments – the targets science says are necessary, the actions needed to meet them, and the external validation of progress.

I have had the privilege of witnessing climate action by activist mayors and their city governments firsthand, through my work as mayor of Toronto, my involvement with the C40 Cities Climate Leadership Group, and involvement in numerous other efforts where cities have worked together or where civil society, business, labor, or academia have worked with cities. Clear to me from all this work is how well cities can learn from each other and adapt the best ideas to their context – as Montreal did creating BIXI bikes after the mayor saw the Paris Vélib' bikeshare program, or as Sydney and Melbourne did after learning about Toronto's Better Buildings Partnership at a global conference of mayors. Perhaps the best example is the founding of the C40 Cities Climate Leadership Group itself.

Founded by London mayor Ken Livingstone in 2005, the idea from inception was that the voices and the actions of the mayors of the world's leading cities could help the world avoid dangerous climate change. The idea wasn't an accident – it came about because of London's development of its own climate strategy. In 2004, Mayor Livingstone, concerned about climate change, tasked his team to develop a city-led climate strategy. This was new to the team, so they turned to colleagues in other cities to find out which cities had leading and innovative ideas on climate. The answer they heard most often was Toronto, and as a result Mayor Livingstone contacted us and asked us to second City of Toronto staff to London to help London create its first climate strategy. The success of this exchange sparked Mayor Livingstone to think about an even bigger idea – what would happen if more cities began to collaborate. After discussion with his peers, the C40 was formed – forty of the largest cities in the world determined to use city-to-city learning and the voices of the mayors of the world's most powerful cities to make a material difference on climate change.

The results have been extraordinary.

Since 2004, the organization has grown, and other collaborative networks are helping to drive urban-based climate action. The Global Covenant of Mayors for Climate and Energy, for example, founded in 2016, has ten thousand members committed to acting on climate change, and activist mayors have championed city action – Mike Bloomberg, my successor as chair of C40, was even made a special advisor to the United Nations secretary general, both in response to his superb contribution as mayor of New York and in acknowledgment of the importance of city governments in addressing the climate crisis.

We know that the actions outlined in this book work and are feasible at scale. At scale, they can go a very long way to getting the world on track to halve emissions by 2030. To do that, we need to act boldly and quickly. Now that the path has been cleared by the mayors of the world's greatest cities, we need those outside the C40 – such as the ten thousand in the Global Covenant – to undertake the same high level of action. Sometimes this will require mayors to act, sometimes it will require other governments to remove barriers to action or to help them act, and sometimes business, labor, and civil society will help to make the change. We know what to do, and the barriers are not ones of technology – they are ones of choice. Will we choose to take effective actions today – actions that we know work because they work today in a major city somewhere in the world – before it is too late?

And that is where individuals come in. People often ask me, "What can I do?"

Here's my answer.

Use Your Voice

Politically, climate action can be challenging. In the early days of the C40, some mayors were acting well ahead of the general consensus of residents of their cities. The pushback is strong from some segments of the fossil fuel industry – such as those who've funded communications campaigns for years to seed doubt about the science (despite the evidence) – which has often made it difficult to take effective climate action. Locally, even measures as simple and effective as adding bike lanes to a busy road can be controversial, and people who support the action must be heard too if the measures are to succeed. The impact of people speaking up can be seen by the rise of global youth movements, like Fridays for Future, whose collective voice has made taking bold climate action far easier, thereby empowering mayors and their city governments to act.

Your voice matters elsewhere as well. Does your employer have a climate plan? What has it done to lower emissions from transport? From buildings it owns or rents? From waste? Does it purchase only clean electricity? Does it have a plan to halve emissions by 2030? Is it actively greening workplaces? Is there an environmental committee at work?

These are all questions worth asking. I have spoken with numerous businesses, government agencies, and other organizations who've decided to act on climate change and I've asked them what motivated them. Uniformly, they mention that their employees demanded change – including new recruits during the interview process. Your voice matters, and collective voices have a massive impact.

Speak up closer to home as well. If you have a friend, neighbor, or relative who still denies the science or who minimizes the risk, speak up. We cannot let those false statements go unchallenged. It doesn't have to be aggressive, but people need to hear from each other in defending what is right.

Use Your Actions

What can you do in your own life? The cliché is that actions speak louder than words. Think about your own life and what you can do to live better and lower your impact on the planet. For example, if you drive a car, do you need to? Can you take transit, walk, or ride? What about where you live? Is it energy efficient?

Are there steps you can take in your home to lower energy consumption from fossil fuels? Can you eat less meat? Create less waste? Fly much less?

My family and I are an example. We no longer own a car and we take transit or walk most of the time. We eat vegetarian meals on weekdays (my wife and daughter all the time), we try to buy less "stuff," and we've taken steps to lower energy consumption in our house. All this has made a difference and helped us lower our impact on the planet, save money, and live more active and healthy lives.

Use Your Vote

Voting matters.

In the last national election in Canada, the central issue was climate change, and of the five parties elected to Parliament, four, including the governing Liberals, were committed to strong climate action. In North America, the main right-wing conservative parties – the Republicans in the United States and the Conservatives in Canada – have chosen to make climate change a partisan issue (given that the root of "conservative" is conserve, I have always found this to be strange). They don't deserve your vote, nor do progressive politicians who say the right thing but don't act. Do your research. Speak up. And reward climate leaders with your support.

The actions discussed in this book have the potential, if adopted at scale globally over the next few years, to put the world back on the path to avoid dangerous climate change. Science shows us that we're running out of time to get on that path and must act now. Cities matter because these proven actions can be implemented while the world collectively grapples with some unanswered questions (such as whether we can remove carbon dioxide from the air) and unproven technologies needed to answer these questions (such as carbon capture at scale).

City-based climate action can make the difference we need now. Which is a good thing. Because not only can we address climate change today – we must.

David Miller
Toronto, Ontario, Canada
April 2020

* * *

Postscript

As I finish writing, most of the world has been shut down due to COVID-19 and the measures needed to prevent its out-of-control spread. But the climate crisis hasn't gone away; if anything, the underlying necessity to act is emphasized by this global pandemic. The importance of city-based solutions has been magnified by the impact of COVID-19, which has been most prevalent in large urban areas. And, like climate change, it has had a disproportionate impact on the least well off in society. Mayors, just as they have on climate, have been working together internationally to learn from each other about the very best ways to address the pandemic. Mayors have shared not only important lessons on response but also supplies of protective equipment, knowledge about testing, and much more. They have created a unique global collaboration on social and economic recovery from the pandemic.

The task they have set themselves is this: How do we, as the leaders of city governments, help lead a recovery that is low carbon, equitable, healthy, and prosperous? How do we use ideas and programs that create work and make our environment better as the basis for a recovery? How do we, as mayors, build these programs at scale in our cities, and how do we influence national and international stimulus programs so that they include these same values of equity, health, sustainability, and shared prosperity?

The mayors and the governments they lead are not waiting to act. Already, Paris, Milan, Seattle, and numerous other cities have made permanent a change to favor active transportation by closing roads to cars and using the space for cycling and walking, thus expediting the plans discussed in Chapter 6. And mayoral leadership has already resulted in national investments in clean public transport, with no doubt more initiatives to come.

Mayors will lead a low-carbon recovery from the pandemic, and that leadership can form the basis of a global economic and social recovery from COVID-19 that puts the world on a path to a low-carbon future. The actions of major cities as outlined in this book – on clean electricity, transport, buildings, and waste – can form the backbone of such a recovery, because they address not only climate but also jobs, equity, and urban quality of life. Those solutions should form the heart of the economic and social recovery needed from COVID-19 – and will show the world the path to solving the climate crisis.

Afterword

In 2015, the nations of the world finally agreed in Paris on a strategy, the Paris Agreement, to address climate change. As mayor of Paris, I have always felt a special responsibility to uphold this agreement. Climate change is scientifically proven and already happening. Its impacts are felt first by the poor and the vulnerable, and therefore it must be addressed to ensure justice and equity as basic human rights.

We – officials, local authorities, and citizens – need above all to recognize the climate emergency and act, even if doing so can be hard. In Paris, when my decisions and policies have come under criticism by media and lobbies, I have been reassured by the support of residents of our city and the global voice of young people demanding for action.

In this task, I have had the privilege of working in partnership with my fellow mayors who take action, learn from one another, and interact with their city administrations, residents, business, industry, and their national governments.

The mayors who are members of the C40 Cities Climate Leadership Group elected me chair from 2016 to 2019; it has been a great honor. During my time as chair, nearly one hundred cities committed to develop and implement plans to keep global average temperature rise to 1.5 degrees, with ambitious action to reduce emissions from transportation, buildings, energy, and waste. Thirty-four of our members monitored their emissions and implemented significant policies. Hundreds of miles of public space were given back to people on foot and on bike, electric buses became commercially feasible, and a lot was accomplished.

We have shown the world the potential for city-based action to dramatically lower greenhouse gas emissions and get the world on track to halve emissions by 2030. However, we must be realistic: our goals will take significant time and effort to achieve.

I truly believe that we can still reach the goals of the Paris Agreement. In the same vein, regional, national, and local governments are mobilized to cope with the global COVID-19 pandemic, and we need to be united and keep our minds open to new ideas, taking the best practices and making them universal, challenging ourselves daily to make our cities healthier, more equitable, and better places to live.

Like David Miller, I am hopeful that we can build this future – not only because it is possible, but because we cannot fail.

Anne Hidalgo
Mayor of Paris
Paris, France
June 2020

Acknowledgments

This book is possible because of the superb leadership of mayors of cities in numerous countries of the world, and because they freely share their ideas and concepts. In turn, the mayors and the city governments they lead would not have been able to succeed without the support, advice, and excellence of the public servants of those cities. In the same way, I am indebted to the University of Waterloo, Faculty of Environmental Studies, for its support; to my publisher, University of Toronto Press, and my editor, Jodi Lewchuk, whose advice and guidance was invaluable; to her colleagues Catherine Plear and Janice Evans, whose talented editing brought this book to completion; and particularly to Heather McDiarmid, my researcher, who, in addition to excellent research, wrote the first drafts of significant parts of several chapters and helped to turn the clear narrative I knew into a substantive book.

Bibliography

Chapter 1: Plans

City of Oslo. (2016). *Climate and Energy Strategy for Oslo*. City of Oslo
Agency for Climate. Retrieved from https://www.klimaoslo.no
/rapporter/english/.

City of Oslo. (2018). *Climate Budget 2019*. City of Oslo Climate Agency.
Retrieved from https://www.klimaoslo.no/rapporter/english/.

Hofstad, H., & Torfing, J. (2017). *Towards a Climate-Resilient City:
Collaborative Innovation for a "Green Shift" in Oslo*. doi:10.1007/978
-3-319-54984-2_10.

Lind, A., & Espegren, K. (2017). "The Use of Energy System Models for
Analysing the Transition to Low-Carbon Cities: The Case of Oslo." *Energy
Strategy Reviews, 15*, 44–56. doi:10.1016/j.esr.2017.01.001.

Nguyen Berg, L.M. (2018). *Oslo's Climate Budget*. Oslo, Norway: C40 Cities.
Retrieved from https://resourcecentre.c40.org/archived-webinars?;&page=4.

Chapter 2: Energy and Electricity

Athen, L., & Baumer, Z. (2018). *Greenhouse Gas Emissions Reduction
Progress Report*. City of Austin. Retrieved from http://austintexas.gov
/sites/default/files/files/Sustainability/030118_FINAL_Memo

_from_OOS_to_MC_RE_Greenhouse_Gas_Emissions_Reduction
_Progress_Report.pdf.

Austin Energy. (2014). *Financial Analysis of Generation Task Force Report and Resolution.* City of Austin.

Austin Energy. (2017). *Austin Energy Resource, Generation and Climate Protection Plan to 2027.* City of Austin. Retrieved from https://austinenergy.com/wcm/connect/6dd1c1c7-77e4-43e4-8789 -838eb9f0790d/2027+Austin+Energy+Resource+Plan+20171002 .pdf?MOD=AJPERES&CVID=lXv4zHS.

Austin Energy. (n.d.). *Our Energy Roadmap.* City of Austin. Retrieved from https://austinenergy.com/wcm/connect/ b08ba414-ce2f-43f8-a78b-676c5583ed73/ourEnergyRoadmap .pdf?MOD=AJPERES&CVID=mNOZAH2.

City of Austin. (2015). *Austin Community Climate Plan 2015.* AustinTexas.gov. Retrieved from http://austintexas.gov/sites/default /files/files/Sustainability/FINAL_-_OOS_AustinClimatePlan _061015.pdf.

City of Austin. (2016). *Austin Community Climate Plan: Phase 1 Implementation Plan.* AustinTexas.gov. Retrieved from https://www .austintexas.gov/sites/default/files/files/ACCP_Implementation _Plan_-_Phase_1_Actions.pdf.

City of Austin. (2019). *Austin Energy.* Retrieved from https:// austinenergy.com.

City of Copenhagen. (2015). *Copenhagen Climate Projects.* Retrieved from https://kk.sites.itera.dk/apps/kk_pub2/pdf/1612_KJz8QrzUpd .pdf.

City of Copenhagen. (n.d.). *CPH 2021 Climate Plan, Short Version English.* Retrieved from https://kk.sites.itera.dk/apps/kk_pub2 /pdf/931_e0pg1K8O8G.pdf.

City of Los Angeles. (2019). *LA's Green New Deal: Sustainable City Plan.* Retrieved from http://plan.lamayor.org/.

Environment America. (2019). *Shining Cities 2019.* Retrieved from https://environmentamerica.org/feature/ame/shining-cities-2019.

Hofor. (n.d.). *District Heating in Copenhagen: Energy-Efficient, Low-Carbon, and Cost-Effective.* Retrieved from https://siteresources

.worldbank.org/ECAEXT/Resources/258598-1279117170185
/7247167-1279119399516/7247361-1279119430793/districtheating
.pdf.

London School of Economics and Political Science. (2014). *Copenhagen
Green Economy Leader Report*. Retrieved from http://www.lse.ac.uk
/cities/publications/research-reports/Copenhagen-Green-Economy
-Leader-Report.

Los Angeles Department of Water and Power. (2013). *Solar Programs*.
Retrieved from https://www.ladwp.com/ladwp/faces/ladwp
/residential/r-savemoney/r-sm-rebatesandprograms/r-sm-rp-solar
?_adf.ctrl-state=q6snhurdl_4&_afrLoop=747131003817342.

Los Angeles Department of Water and Power. (2018). *LADWP 2017–2018
Power Infrastructure Plan*. Retrieved from https://s3-us-west-2
.amazonaws.com/ladwp-jtti/wp-content/uploads/sites/3/2018/07
/11111628/2018-Power-Infrastructure-Plan1.pdf.

Los Angeles Department of Water and Power. (2019). *LADWP
Shared Solar Guidelines*. Retrieved from https://www.ladwp.com
/cs/idcplg?IdcService=GET_FILE&dDocName
=OPLADWPCCB675089&RevisionSelectionMethod
=LatestReleased.

Mitsubishi Hitachi Power Systems America Inc., Magnum Development.
(2019). *World's Largest Renewable Energy Storage Project Announced
in Utah*. Retrieved from https://magnumdev.com/wp-content
/uploads/2019/05/NEWS-RELEASE-MHPS-Magnum-Partnership
-05-30-19-FINAL.pdf.

Pecan Street. (2019). *Pecan Street*. Retrieved from https://www
.pecanstreet.org/.

Roth, S. (2019, July 11). "Los Angeles Is Finally Ditching Coal and
Replacing It with Another Polluting Fuel." *Los Angeles Times*. Retrieved
from https://www.latimes.com/business/la-fi-utah-coal-los-angeles
-climate-20190711-story.html.

Roth, S. (2019, August 7). "A Clean Energy Breakthrough Could Be
Buried Deep below Rural Utah." *Los Angeles Times*. Retrieved from
https://www.latimes.com/environment/story/2019-08-07
/renewable-energy-storage-los-angeles.

State of Green. (2018). *District Energy: Energy Efficiency for Urban Areas.* Retrieved from http://dbdh.dk/wp-content/uploads/8855.pdf.

Chapter 3: Existing Buildings

C40 Cities. (2015). "Tokyo's Urban Cap and Trade Scheme Delivers Substantial Carbon Reductions." Retrieved from https://www.c40 .org/case_studies/tokyo-s-urban-cap-and-trade-scheme-delivers -substantial-carbon-reductions.

City in Sight. (n.d.). *Projected Changes in Annual Emissions.* Retrieved from http://cityinsight-interface.ssg.coop/toronto-emissions.

City of New York. (2018). *New York City Municipal Government Energy Benchmarking Results 2017.* Retrieved from https://www1.nyc.gov /assets/finance/downloads/pdf/benchmarking/2017_energy _benchmarking_results.pdf.

City of New York. (n.d.a). *One City Built to Last.* Retrieved from https:// www1.nyc.gov/site/builttolast/index.page.

City of New York. (n.d.b). *One City Built to Last: Technical Working Group Report.* Retrieved from https://www1.nyc.gov/assets/sustainability /downloads/pdf/publications/TWGreport_04212016.pdf.

City of Sydney. (2015). *Energy Efficiency Master Plan 2015–2030.* Retrieved from https://www.cityofsydney.nsw.gov.au/__data/assets /pdf_file/0020/241436/Energy-Efficiency-Master-Plan-low-res.pdf.

City of Sydney. (2017). *Environmental Action 2016–2021 Strategy and Action Plan.* Retrieved from https://www.cityofsydney.nsw.gov.au /vision/sustainable-sydney-2030/sustainability.

City of Sydney. (n.d.). *Greening Your Business.* Retrieved from https:// www.cityofsydney.nsw.gov.au/business/build-your-skills-and -knowledge/business-programs/greening-your-business.

City of Toronto. (2019a). *Environmental Grants and Incentives.* Retrieved from https://www.toronto.ca/services-payments/water-environment /environmental-grants-incentives-2/.

City of Toronto. (2019b). *Transform TO.* Retrieved from https://www .toronto.ca/services-payments/water-environment/environmentally -friendly-city-initiatives/transformto/.

City of Toronto & Live Green Toronto. (n.d.). *Toronto Environmental Progress Report 2016*. Retrieved from https://www.toronto.ca/services-payments/water-environment/environmentally-friendly-city-initiatives/reports-plans-policies-research/environmental-progress-report/.

Hughes, S., Yordi, S., & Besco, L. (2018). "The Role of Pilot Projects in Urban Climate Change Policy Innovation." *Policy Studies Journal, 48*(2). doi:10.1111/psj.12288.

International Carbon Action Partnership. (2019). *Japan – Tokyo Cap-and-Trade Program*. International Carbon Action Partnership. Retrieved from https://icapcarbonaction.com/en/?option=com_etsmap&task=export&format=pdf&layout=list&systems%5B%5D=51.

Nishida, Y., Hua, Y., & Okamoto, N. (2016). "Alternative Building Emission-Reduction Measure: Outcomes from the Tokyo Cap-and-Trade Program." *Building Research & Information, 44*(5–6), 644–59. doi:10.1080/09613218.2016.1169475.

Tokyo Metropolitan Government. (2011). *On the Path to a Low Carbon City: Tokyo Climate Change Strategy*. Tokyo Metropolitan Government Bureau of Environment. Retrieved from http://www.kankyo.metro.tokyo.jp/en/climate/index.html.

Tokyo Metropolitan Government. (2018). *Final Energy and Greenhouse Gas Emission in Tokyo (FY2015)*. Tokyo Metropolitan Government Bureau of Environment. Retrieved from http://www.kankyo.metro.tokyo.jp/en/climate/index.html.

Tokyo Metropolitan Government. (2019). *Results of Tokyo Cap-and-Trade Program in the 8th Fiscal Year*. Tokyo Metropolitan Government Bureau of Environment. Retrieved from http://www.kankyo.metro.tokyo.jp/en/climate/cap_and_trade/index.html.

Toronto Atmospheric Fund. (2018). *Robert Cooke Co-op Case Study*. Retreived from https://taf.ca/publications/robert-cooke-co-op-case-study-towerwise-retrofit-project/.

TowerWise. (2019). *Finance*. Retrieved from https://taf.ca/programs/towerwise/.

Transform TO. (2016). *Climate Actions for a Healthy, Equitable, and Prosperous Toronto: Report 1 Short-Term Strategies – Highlights*. Retrieved from https://www.toronto.ca/wp-content/uploads/2018/02/9488-TransformTO_Report1-Highlights.pdf.

Transform TO. (2017). *2050 Pathway to a Low Carbon Toronto: Report 2 Highlights of the City of Toronto Staff Report*. Retrieved from https://www.toronto.ca/wp-content/uploads/2017/10/91c7-TransformTO-2050-Pathway-to-a-Low-Carbon-Toronto-Highlights-Report.pdf.

Chapter 4: New Buildings

C40 Cities. (n.d.). *Net Zero Carbon Buildings Declaration*. Retrieved from https://www.c40.org/other/net-zero-carbon-buildings-declaration.

City of Cape Town. (2015). *Cape Town Energy 2040 Vision*. Retrieved from https://www.esi-africa.com/wp-content/uploads/2016/05/Sarah-Ward.pdf.

City of Los Angeles. (2019). *LA's Green New Deal: Sustainable City Plan*. Retrieved from http://plan.lamayor.org/.

City of New York. (n.d.). *One City Built to Last: Technical Working Group Report*. Retrieved from https://www1.nyc.gov/assets/sustainability/downloads/pdf/publications/TWGreport_04212016.pdf.

City of Tshwane. (2009). *City of Tshwane Green Building Development Policy*. Retrieved from http://www.cityenergy.org.za/uploads/resource_312.pdf.

City of Tshwane. (n.d.). *Climate Response Strategy*. Retrieved from http://www.cityenergy.org.za/uploads/resource_472.pdf.

City of Vancouver. (2016). *Zero Emissions Building Plan*. Retrieved from https://vancouver.ca/green-vancouver/zero-emissions-buildings.aspx.

City of Vancouver. (2019). *Climate Emergency Response*. Retrieved from https://vancouver.ca/green-vancouver/climate-emergency-response.aspx.

Energy Step Code. (2019). *Energy Step Code: Building beyond the Standard*. Retrieved from https://energystepcode.ca/.

Global Covenant of Mayors. (2019). *Global Covenant of Mayors for Climate and Energy*. Retrieved from https://www.globalcovenantofmayors.org.

Gonchar, J. (2016). *Continuing Education: The Kathleen Grimm School for Leadership and Sustainability at Sandy Ground*. Architectural Record. Retrieved from https://www.architecturalrecord.com/articles/11407

-continuing-education-the-kathleen-grimm-school-for-leadership
-and-sustainability-at-sandy-ground.

New York City Mayor's Office of Sustainability. (2019). *One NYC 2050 Building a Strong and Fair City*, Volume 1. Retrieved from https:// onenyc.cityofnewyork.us/.

Som. (2016). *The Making of New York's Greenest School*. Retrieved from https://medium.com/@SOM/the-making-of-new-york-s-greenest -school-93dc20322ac4#.s9j0xgwbc.

Chapter 5: Public Transportation and Chapter 6: Personal and Other Transportation

Asian Development Bank. (2018). *Sustainable Transport Solutions: Low Carbon Buses in the People's Republic of China*. http://dx.doi.org /10.22617/TCS189646-2. Retrieved from https://www.adb .org/publications/sustainable-transport-solutions-peoples-republic -china.

ATM. (2018). *Milan Is Going Green*.

ATM. (2019). *Milan Public Transport Operator Company Information*.

Bianchi Alves, B., Sethi, K., Lopez Dodero, A., Hoyos Guerrero, A., Puga, D., Yeghyaian Valls, E., ... Qiu, Y. (2019). *Green Your Ride: Clean Buses in Latin America – Summary Report*. World Bank Group. Retrieved from http://documents.worldbank.org/curated/en /410331548180859451/Green-Your-Bus-Ride-Clean-Buses-in -Latin-America-Summary-Report.

Bloomberg New Energy Finance. (2018). *Electric Buses in Cities: Driving towards Cleaner Air and Lower CO2*. Bloomberg Finance L.P. Retrieved from https://data.bloomberglp.com/professional /sites/24/2018/05/Electric-Buses-in-Cities-Report-BNEF-C40-Citi .pdf.

Breathelife. (2017, January 24). Interview with Marcelo Mena, Chile's Minister of the Environment. Retrieved from https://breathelife2030 .org/news/marcelo-mena-qa/.

Centre for Public Impact. (2016, April 7). *Light Rail Transit in Addis Ababa*. Retrieved from https://www.centreforpublicimpact.org /case-study/light-rail-transit-in-addis-ababa/.

C40 Cities. (2016). *Case Study: Addis Ababa BRT System – Stakeholder Engagement Series.* Retrieved from https://c40-production-images .s3.amazonaws.com/case_studies/images/278_C40_Addis_Ababa _Case_Study.original.pdf?1480503661.

C40 Cities. (2017). *Addis Ababa Light Rail Transit Project.* Retrieved from https://www.c40.org/awards/2016-awards/profiles/107.

City of London. (2019). *London Electric Vehicle Infrastructure Delivery Plan.* Retrieved from http://lruc.content.tfl.gov.uk/london-electric -vehicle-infrastructure-taskforce-delivery-plan-executive-summary.pdf.

City of Paris. (2018). *Paris Climate Action Plan.* Retrieved from https:// api-site-cdn.paris.fr/images/101081.

Climate Action. (2017, June 21). "Chile's Largest Metro Network to Be Powered by Solar and Wind." Retrieved from http://www .climateaction.org/news/chiles-largest-metro-network-to-be -powered-by-solar-and-wind.

Dong et al. (2018). "Towards a Low Carbon Transition of Urban Public Transport in Megacities: A Case Study of Shenzhen, China." *Resources, Conservation & Recycling, 134,* 149–55. Retrieved from https://doi.org /10.1016/j.resconrec.2018.03.011.

Edwards, G., Viscidi, L., & Mojica, C. (2018). *Charging Ahead: The Growth of Electric Car and Bus Markets in Latin American Cities.* The Dialogue. Retrieved from https://www.thedialogue.org/analysis /charging-ahead-the-growth-of-electric-car-and-bus-markets-in-latin -american-cities/.

"ENGIE to Provide 100 Electric Buses in Santiago, Chile by 2019." (2018, October 16). *ENP Newswire.* Retrieved from https://link.gale .com/apps/doc/A558369516/AONE?u=uniwater&sid=AONE &xid=35967238.

Gallardo, L., et al. (2018). "Evolution of Air Quality in Santiago: The Role of Mobility and Lessons from the Science-Policy Interface." *Elementa: Science of the Anthropocene, 6,* 38. https://doi.org/10.1525 /elementa.293.

Institute for Transportation and Development Policy. (2019a). *Santiago*. Retrieved from https://www.itdp.org/city-transformations /santiago/.

Institute for Transportation and Development Policy. (2019b). *Sustainable Transport Award 2017: Santiago, Chile*. Retrieved from https://staward .org/winners/2017-santiago-chile/.

Lehe, L. (2019). "Downtown Congestion Pricing in Practice." *Transportation Research Part C: Emerging Technologies, 100*, 200–23. doi:10.1016/j.trc.2019.01.020.

Lu Lu, Lulu Xue, & Weimin Zhou. (2018). "How Did Shenzhen, China, Build the World's Biggest Electric Bus Fleet?" World Resource Institute. Retrieved from https://www.wri.org/blog/2018/04 /how-did-shenzhen-china-build-world-s-largest-electric-bus-fleet.

Mayor of London. (2018). *London Environment Strategy*. Greater London Authority. Retrieved from https://www.london.gov.uk/sites /default/files/london_environment_strategy_0.pdf.

Merino, T. (2019, August 9). "Santiago's Electric Bus Fleet Cuts Costs and Cleans the Air." *Bloomberg Businessweek*. Retrieved from https://www.bloomberg.com/news/features/2019-08-09/santiago -s-electric-bus-fleet-cuts-costs-and-cleans-the-air.

Metz, D. (2018). "Tackling Urban Traffic Congestion: The Experience of London, Stockholm and Singapore." *Case Studies on Transport Policy, 6*(4), 494–8. doi:10.1016/j.cstp.2018.06.002.

Morton, C., Lovelace, R., & Anable, J. (2017). "Exploring the Effect of Local Transport Policies on the Adoption of Low Emission Vehicles: Evidence from the London Congestion Charge and Hybrid Electric Vehicles." *Transport Policy 60*, 34–46. doi:10.1016/j.tranpol.2017 .08.007.

Nallet, Clelie. (2018). "The Challenge of Urban Mobility: A Case Study of Addis Ababa Light Rail, Ethiopia." Ifri.org. Retrieved from https:// www.ifri.org/en/publications/notes-de-lifri/challenge-urban-mobility -case-study-addis-ababa-light-rail-ethiopia.

O'Sullivan, F. (2018, October 10). *A City That Takes Climate Change Seriously: Paris*. Citylab. Retrieved from https://www.citylab.com /environment/2018/10/paris-preparing-warming-world/572506/.

Paris. (2015). *Paris à vélo*. Retrieved from https://www.paris.fr/pages /paris-a-velo-225.

Paris. (2017a). *Piétonnisation des Berges rive droite: un air de meilleure qualité*. Retrieved from https://www.paris.fr/actualites/pietonnisation -des-berges-rive-droite-un-air-de-meilleure-qualite-4439.

Paris. (2017b). *Piétonnisation des Berges rive droite: pourquoi le projet est pertinent*. Retrieved from https://www.paris.fr/berges.

Paris. (2020). *Budget participatif.* Retrieved from https:// budgetparticipatif.paris.fr/bp/.

Paris. (n.d.). *Paris capitale du vélo*. Retrieved from https://cdn.paris.fr /paris/2019/07/24/7e17b7493fc5b8838b064ae502184a50.pdf.

Phys.org. (2019). *Giving Up Gas: China's Shenzhen Switches to Electric Taxis*. Retrieved from https://phys.org/news/2019-01-gas-china -shenzhen-electric-taxis.html.

Santiago Times, The. (2017, November 22). "Transantiago's First Pure Electric Buses Hit the Roads." *The Santiago Times*. Retrieved from https://santiagotimes.cl/2017/11/22/transantiagos-first-pure -electric-buses-hit-the-roads/.

Santiago Times, The. (2019a, January 22). "Chile Adds Another 100 Electric Buses to Its Fleet." *The Santiago Times*. Retrieved from https://santiagotimes.cl/2019/01/22/chile-adds-another-100 -electric-buses-to-its-fleet/.

Santiago Times, The. (2019b, March 28). "Chile Doubles Santiago's Electric Bus Fleet." *The Santiago Times.* Retrieved from https:// santiagotimes.cl/2019/03/28/chile-doubles-santiagos-electric -bus-fleet/.

Saurabh. (2017, July 8). "Chile's Santiago Metro Will Meet 60% of Its Energy Demand from Renewables." CleanTechnica. Retrieved from https://cleantechnica.com/2017/07/08/chiles-santiago-metro -will-meet-60-energy-demand-renewables/.

Tanguy, Y. (2018, February 21). "Paris: fermeture des voies sur berges – La Mairie de Paris fait appel de la décision et prend un nouvel arrêté de piétonnisation." LCI Société. Retrieved from https://www.lci.fr/societe /paris-fermeture-des-voies-sur-berges-la-mairie-de-paris-fait-appel -de-la-decision-et-prend-un-nouvel-arrete-de-pietonnisation -2079448.html.

Tarrosy, I., & Voros, Z. (2019, January 26). "Revisiting Chinese Transportation Projects in Ethiopia." *The Diplomat*. Retrieved from https://thediplomat.com/2019/01/revisiting-chinese-transportation-projects-in-ethiopia/.

Transport for London. (2019). *Driving*. Retrieved from https://tfl.gov.uk/modes/driving/.

Willsher, K. (2017, January 8). "Paris Mayor Unveils Plan to Restrict Traffic and Pedestrianise City Centre." *The Guardian*. Retrieved from https://www.theguardian.com/world/2017/jan/08/paris-mayor-anne-hidalgo-plan-restrict-traffic-pedestrianise-city-centre-france.

Willsher, K. (2019, June 7). "Eiffel Tower Revamp to Turn Roads into Garden in Heart of Paris." *The Guardian*. Retrieved from https://www.theguardian.com/world/2019/jun/07/eiffel-tower-revamp-to-turn-roads-into-garden-in-heart-of-paris.

World Bank. (2019). *Green Your Bus Ride, Clean Buses in Latin America Summary Report*. Retrieved from http://documents.worldbank.org/curated/en/410331548180859451/pdf/133929-WP-PUBLIC-P164403-Summary-Report-Green-Your-Bus-Ride.pdf.

Chapter 7: Waste

City of Ljubljana. (2019a). *Towards Circular Economy*. Retrieved from https://www.ljubljana.si/en/ljubljana-for-you/environmental-protection/towards-circular-economy/.

City of Ljubljana. (2019b). *City of Ljubljana*. Retrieved from https://www.ljubljana.si/en/.

Dakskobler, L. (2019, May 23). "From No Recycling to Zero Waste: How Ljubljana Rethought Its Rubbish." *The Guardian*. Retrieved from https://www.theguardian.com/cities/2019/may/23/zero-recycling-to-zero-waste-how-ljubljana-rethought-its-rubbish.

MacBride, S. (2013, December 6). *San Francisco's Famous 80% Diversion Rate: Anatomy of an Exemplar*. Discard Studies. Retrieved from https://discardstudies.com/2013/12/06/san-franciscos-famous-80-waste-diversion-rate-anatomy-of-an-exemplar/.

Oblak, E. (2019). *The Story of Ljubljana: Case Study #5*. Zero Waste Europe. Retrieved from https://zerowasteeurope.eu/downloads /case-study-5-ljubljana-2/.

San Francisco Planning Department. (2017). *2017 Greenhouse Gas Reduction Strategy Update*. Retrieved from http://sfmea.sfplanning.org /GHG/GHG_Strategy_October2017.pdf.

SF Environment. (n.d.). *SF Environment*. Retrieved from https:// sfenvironment.org.

Index

Note: Page numbers in bold indicate figures, photographs, or captions.

100, 110; clean electricity, 93;
density, 91; financing, 96–7; Los
Angeles, 94
Recology, 141–2
recycling, 139–40, **140**, 141, 142–3,
144–5, 146, 147, 149
Regis Towers Complex, 65
Rensselaer Polytechnic Institute, 88
Republican Party (US), and climate
change, 156
retro-commissioning. *See* energy
retrofits
Ridership Growth Strategy, 101–2
right sizing, of vehicles, 129
Rio de Janeiro, Brazil, climate agenda,
16–17
Robert Cooke Co-op, 61

Safe Drug Disposal Stewardship
Ordinance, 143
San Francisco, waste management,
140–6; apartment buildings,
144–5; assistance, 145; within city
departments, 145; construction
waste, 145; mandatory recycling
and composting, 143–5; motivation,
141; packaging bans, 142; planning,
140–1; producer responsibility,
142–3, 146; Recology, 141–2; zero-
waste facility, 146
Santiago, Chile, bus service, 106–8
Sao Paolo, Brazil, methane-capture
system, 146
Seine Quayside, 125
sewers, xiv, 36, 75
Shared Solar Program, 34

Shenzhen, China: buses, 104–5, **105**;
electric taxis, 130–1
skyscrapers, 88–9
Small Scale Energy Generation
Program, 31
Smart Green Apartments, 65
smog, 2–3, **3**, 102, 106
Snaga (waste-management company),
147
solar energy: advantages, 26–7; electric
vehicle charging, 107; Exhibition
Place, 23, 24; Kathleen Grimm
School, 87, 88; Los Angeles, 32–5;
rooftop, **29**, 30–1, 86–7; solar gain,
77; solar wall, 77; thermal hot-water
heaters, 5; Toronto, 59; utility scale,
28, 32, 35. *See also* electricity;
wind energy
Solar Rooftops Program, 34
solutions, individuals: actions, use of,
156; voice, use of, 155–6; votes, use
of, 156–7
Soundranayagam, Princely, 144
South African cities, and passive
design, 76–7
Sowah, Mohammed Adjei, 149, 150
split-incentive problem, 47, 48, 66, 74
sprawl, urban, 112
St James' Hall, 66
standards, conventional, 72
standards, green, 72–8
standards, Passive House, 79–80
storytelling, as strategy, 14
superblocks, 20–1
Sydney, Better Buildings Partnership,
63–6

David Miller is the Director of International Diplomacy and Global Ambassador of Inclusive Climate Action at C40 Cities Climate Leadership Group. He is responsible for supporting nearly 100 mayors of the world's largest cities in their climate leadership and building a global movement for socially equitable action to mitigate and adapt to climate change. He served as Chair of C40 Cities from 2008 until 2010.

Miller was Mayor of Toronto from 2003 to 2010. Under his leadership, Toronto became widely admired internationally for its environmental leadership, economic strength, and social integration. He is a leading advocate for the creation of sustainable urban economies and a strong and forceful champion for the next generation of jobs through sustainability. Miller has held a variety of public and private positions and served as Future of Cities Global Fellow at the Polytechnic Institute of New York University from 2011 to 2014.

Miller is a Harvard-trained economist and professionally a lawyer.